I thought we had forever

Carlette Patterson

Contributing Authors:
Steve, Amanda, Sara, and Makena Patterson

I Thought We Had Forever Copyright 2011 © Carlette Patterson

ISBN 978-0-9848151-0-4

Library of Congress Control Number: 2011961155

All rights reserved. No part of this book may be reproduced in any form without written permission from the publisher and author. Except for the use in any review, the reproduction or utilization of this work in whole or in part in any form by an electronic, mechanical or other means, now know or hereafter invented, photocopying and recording, or in any information storage or retrieval system, is forbidden without the written permission of the publisher and author.

All photographs courtesy of the author.

Cover Design: Jack Sullivan

Published by: Patterson Sports Ventures 602-468-9700

To Steve, from his little women

CONTENTS

INTRODUCTION

Chapter One	Roots And Wings	1
Chapter Two	Faith	8
Chapter Three	Amanda's Story	11
Chapter Four	Sara's Story	15
Chapter Five	When Does Forever Begin?	17
Chapter Six	C	19
Chapter Seven	Love	25
Chapter Eight	Frozen Pizza and Wine	26
Chapter Nine	Surviving Life	28
Chapter Ten	Our Summer Project	33
Chapter Eleven	Time To Say Good-Bye	36
Chapter Twelve	July 28, 2004, Dear Steve	40
Chapter Thirteen	Now What?	43
Chapter Fourteen	Monterey	45
Chapter Fifteen	A Very Thin Veil	48
Chapter Sixteen	Steve's Story	52
Chapter Seventeen	UCLA Reunion	61
Chapter Eighteen	Six O'clock	63
Chapter Nineteen	Daddy Day	66
Chapter Twenty	Too Much Pain	70
Chapter Twenty-One	Remodel of a Lifetime	73
Chapter Twenty-Two	Touching the Pain	76
Chapter Twenty-Three	I Love You, Steve	78
Chapter Twenty-Four	Love Hurts	80
Chapter Twenty-Five	The Holidays	84

Chapter Twenty-Six	Only By the Grace of God	87
Chapter Twenty-Seven	Getting Real ... Real Pearls	90
Chapter Twenty-Eight	Good-Bye, USA, Hello, South Africa	92
Chapter Twenty-Nine	Hi, Mom, It's Me!	96
Chapter Thirty	My Faith	104
Chapter Thirty-One	Valentine's Day	105
Chapter Thirty-Two	Death, You Are So Cruel	108
Chapter Thirty-Three	Day By Day	110
Chapter Thirty-Four	One Year Without Forever	112
Chapter Thirty-Five	Love Blesses	117
Chapter Thirty-Six	More Reality	121
Chapter Thirty-Seven	Makena's Love Notes to Her Daddy	128
Chapter Thirty-Eight	Finding Hope	135
Chapter Thirty-Nine	Amanda's Turn	136
Chapter Forty	Daddy Day Love Notes from Sara	140
Chapter Forty-One	Talking to God in New Zealand	150
Chapter Forty-Two	Cupcakes and Philanthropy	154
Chapter Forty-Three	Road Trip, Tears, and Love	159
Chapter Forty-Four	The Gift of Friendships	162
Chapter Forty-Five	Our First Family Picture	172
Chapter Forty-Six	Someday...Italy	174
Chapter Forty-Seven	Forgiveness	177
Chapter Forty-Eight	Never Give Up, Where We Are Today	179
Chapter Forty-Nine	And the Greatest of These Is Love	188
Chapter Fifty	Simple Words Worth Striving to Live By 1 Corinthians 13:4	192

INTRODUCTION

A photograph, a letter, a word spoken—they each tell an intimate story, and within our stories are moments that change our lives forever. I've learned that I have no idea what each day will bring. I don't know what phone call or message I'll receive or what person I'll bump into that will change my direction or deliver a new thought to me.

I Thought We Had Forever is a collection of love letters, journal entries, and e-mails written by our family as we found our way through life, searching to figure out what love is. These writings make up chapters of our life story and reveal how God is present in every detail.

This is not a perfect story. It includes divorce, blended family issues, drug abuse, broken hearts, and shattered dreams. Our family struggles through death, through grief, through healing, and through faith as we find our way to love. Along the way, God helps us find pieces of our hearts that he knew long before we were even aware they were a possibility. What a journey life is. Our family has discovered that as long as our bags are packed with love, God will take care of all the other details. To him be the glory.

It amazes me that something so valuable—our life—is created by a million pieces of destiny falling into place at just the right time. My life has all the components I hoped for, yet they were all given to me in a very different way than I could have ever imagined. What I thought was a mistake was exactly what I needed to lead me to the next moment that became a valuable chapter in my life story.

I have learned to honor the days that have become my life, and in this book, I share them with you. As you turn the pages of my life, I hope that you find pieces of you that have been hidden from your sight but locked into your memory.

I hope my words and my story inspire you to love—to love God, to love yourself, to love your life, and to go for the love you have always wanted. If you can find the courage to love, you will be able to experience a depth of emotion, both good and bad, that somehow through the twists and turns that life takes will lead you to your true self.

CHAPTER ONE
Roots and Wings

I can remember every detail of some of the moments that changed my life, including the weather, the sounds, the smells, and even what I was wearing. For other life-changing moments, I can only remember a fleeting thought coming to consciousness and then dismissing it because I didn't think it was important. Ah, but now as I look back at my life, I see how very important those thoughts were and wonder what my life would be like if I had paid attention to them. Those moments have become my story, and now, many years later, they mean so much more because they reveal how I got to be me. . .

I was five years old. I loved playing dolls. Every Christmas, my Grandmother Lewis gave me a new doll. The moment I unwrapped that present, I fell in love. I named my new doll and welcomed her to my family. I spent all my time playing dolls and couldn't wait to wake up every morning to take care of them. I would run home from school for lunch just so I could feed them. I spent all afternoon playing dolls until it was time for bed. I would dress them all in their jammies, tuck each one in, say their prayers, and then go to sleep so I could wake up and do it all over again.

I was eight years old. I spent my summers at the public swimming pool. I loved swimming. Every morning, as soon as I woke up, I would ride my purple bike to the pool and wait outside the gate for it to open. They hosted swimming lessons in the mornings, so I took as many lessons as possible just so I could swim all morning. Lunch time was an hour break. I would ride my bike home, eat as fast as I could, and then ride back to wait for the gate to open for free swim time. The pool closed at 4:00 for the swim team to practice. I was always disappointed when the lifeguard blew the final whistle for everyone to get out and go home. By the middle of the summer, I had passed the Senior Lifesaving class — the most advanced class offered — so I didn't know what lessons I was going to take to be able to keep swimming in the mornings. The swim coach was the Senior Lifesaving class instructor, and she asked me if I wanted to join the swim team. I didn't even know what that meant. She told me about the practice times—three times a day—and that sounded fun. I went home and asked my mom if I could join. She asked me if I wanted to. I wasn't sure, so I asked my brother; he was my hero and knew everything. He said, "No way! Swimming is boring. You just swim back and forth all the time. Who would want to do that? Not me." So I said, "No way, I don't want to join the swim team because it's boring. You just swim back and forth all the time. Who would want to do that? Not me." A couple weeks passed, and the coach asked again. This time, I said yes. The next year, I was state champion in several events. I spent the next ten years swimming until I finished my career at Arizona State University.

I was ten years old. My brother, Steve, who was five years older than me, got his first pickup and named it the Green Phantom. The Green Phantom became our office for our first business. Our family owned a sheep ranch a couple hours from the town of Artesia, New Mexico, where we lived. We took orders from the neighbors for firewood. On the weekends, we would drive to the ranch, load up the Green Phantom with wood, and bring back as many orders as possible. As we pulled up to each neighbor's house, I would jump in the back of the pickup, put on my gloves, and prepare to hand the wood to Steve for him to stack it up. We would time ourselves to see how fast we could get it unloaded. I don't remember how fast we did it, but I do remember feeling so proud of the work we had done once that last piece of wood was perfectly stacked. As we drove away, we would high-five each other.

In December, we would take orders for Christmas trees. I loved that. Steve and I would head to the ranch and spend all day driving around to find our neighbors their perfect tree. We would talk about whose tree it was going to be, review our notes detailing what they wanted, and then begin the search. We had to make sure we found trees for every family on our list by dark, because once the sun went down, our work day was over. As the sun set, the Green Phantom looked like our sleigh, piled high with Christmas trees. I loved the feeling of heading back to town to deliver each family their hand-picked tree. We would ring the doorbell, bring in the tree, and watch as the whole family got excited about how pretty it was.

Those days in the Green Phantom became my classroom. I learned so much about the joy of doing meaningful work. The firewood, the Christmas trees, the long drives to the ranch—it could have just been a way to make some extra cash, but my brother made it about so much more than that. I don't remember how much money I made, but I remember what it felt like to take pride in my work, to pay attention to every detail, and to deliver the perfect product to each neighbor. Today, Steve and I have moved on to many other business ventures, but we still treat every client like we're picking out their family Christmas tree.

I was thirteen years old. I had lived away from home most of my childhood because I had moved to different cities to train with swim coaches who could help me achieve my goal of making the Olympics. Because we lived in a small town that did not have an indoor swimming facility, I had to move to a larger city to be able to train in swimming year-round. At first my mom moved with me. We got an apartment and lived four hours away from my dad. Every day, I went to swimming early in the morning, to school all day, and then to swimming in the evening. Once that school year ended, my mom moved back home and I moved in with relatives for the summer. When I did not have a swim meet on the weekends, which was not very often, I was able to go home and see my dad. For years, this was my normal, to spend most of my time living with friends, relatives, or even my coaches, so that I could train year round. School, relationships, everything became second to training.

Life was lonely, intense, competitive, and filled only with the pursuit of winning. The more I won, the more pressure came to keep winning. Family time consisted of my parents driving me to swim meets. Weekends were spent competing, and life revolved around how I could be a better swimmer. I longed for fun, friendships, and someone to care about who I was other than Carlette the competitive swimmer. I wanted more than swimming in my life, so I tried out for my school sports teams and added playing volleyball and basketball to the things I liked to do.

I was fourteen years old. I was standing in front of the mirror getting ready for prom. I was a sophomore in high school, attending boarding school. I was going to the prom with a junior. I could see the reflection of my dress hanging on my closet door. The air was filled with excitement and the thrill of what the night would bring. There was a knock on my door. My dorm mother said I had a phone call. It was my mom. My Granddaddy Lewis had died of a heart attack. It had only been weeks since my spring break, when I had gone home and we had spent time as a family laughing and just being together. Within hours, I was on a plane flying home. My uncle picked up my brother from college, me from the airport, and we made the long drive home. It was so sad to see Grandmother Lewis alone. *Why would*

God do this? I wondered. *How can life change so suddenly, so fast?* The stability of my life broke into little pieces. Things I had thought were permanent were now gone.

I was very close to my Grandmother and Granddaddy Lewis. To my Granddaddy, I was his Blonde. He loved me and loved me and loved me — no matter what. Growing up, when I had to sell Girl Scout cookies, he would ask me how many I had to sell and then write me a check so I wouldn't have to do all the hard work of selling them. Delivering the cookies was simple too; they all went to Granddaddy's house. I have no idea what he did with all those cookies. When I read him articles in the paper about me and my swimming accomplishments, he would gently wipe away the tears that rolled down his cheek under his glasses. He would hug me and tell me how proud of me he was. I loved those hugs. When I spent the night with my grandparents, I would wake up to waffles smothered in whip cream, butter, and syrup. Not just any syrup — Grandmother would make prickly pear syrup from the prickly pears on the cactus at our ranch. I don't remember much about the taste, but I do remember how pretty the bright pink syrup was. After I got dressed for the day, having slipped on a pair of jeans, Granddaddy would slip a dollar bill in my pocket. He would say that if my jeans were too tight for him to slip some money in my back pocket, my jeans were too tight. Since I traveled so much for swimming and now was away at boarding school, I called them every Sunday morning, collect, and we would tell each other how much we loved each other.

It was my Grandmother Lewis that taught me about God. She was my Sunday school teacher. We lived in a small town and went to a very small church; I was the only one in Sunday school. Every Sunday, I would sit at a little black table with her, and she would tell me all about our amazing God and how much he loved me. I learned to love God because it was such a special part of my relationship with my grandmother. When I thought about God, I thought about Grandmother Lewis, and I thought about love.

I was sixteen years old. I was sitting on an airplane going to San Francisco to visit my roommate from boarding school. A guy sat next to me. We got engaged ten months later.

I was seventeen years old. I had found someone who would care about me as a wife, not a swimmer. I was tired of life revolving around training, competing, winning, and losing. I knew there had to be more to life than swimming. It was easy to give up the dream of being in the Olympics because it felt more like other people's dream for my life than mine. My parents and coaches were extremely disappointed in me, but I was done. I wanted to be loved much more than I wanted to win. I didn't know what love felt like or meant, but I knew I wanted it.

My soon-to-be husband was twenty-five years old. He was established in a career and promised me the world. He promised to take care of me and assured me I would want for nothing in life. We could have children; I could stay home with them and live happily ever after. It all seemed like a fairytale, and I so wanted to believe him, but at times he said and did things that didn't feel right. I convinced myself that it felt better than going back to college and continuing my swimming career. I didn't think about options; I just continued planning the wedding and telling myself that all my doubts were normal. I didn't want to be wrong about getting married because I really wanted a different life. Things weren't perfect in our relationship, but what was perfect? So why question it? I knew nothing about being in a relationship, so I was sure that if I just did everything he wanted, I would be able to make it work.

I was eighteen years old. I was going to be a mom. Life couldn't get any better. I had wanted to be a mom my whole life. I felt so blessed. Amanda arrived in February.

I was nineteen years old. Another gift of love due to arrive in October. Sara was born.

I was twenty years old. I was married to a man who mentally and physically abused me. Life appeared to be perfect from the outside, but the abuse on the inside was becoming unbearable. I tried everything to convince myself that it wasn't so bad and that I could endure anything for my girls. The more I endured, the worse it got. I found that the only way to cope was to lose myself. After all, I didn't really matter anymore. All that mattered was taking care of Amanda and Sara. I felt that I had gotten myself into the situation; I had ignored all the signs and the feeling that something wasn't right, so whatever pain came with that, I deserved. I would work harder to be a better wife. I would change. I would act differently. I would make sure that whatever my husband wanted, I would give him. My feelings, my thoughts—they had to be all wrong. *Otherwise,* I thought, *why would this be happening to me?*

As much as I tried to change, to be the person that my husband wanted me to be, nothing stopped the fighting, the harsh words, the anxiety of not knowing when I was going to do something that would make him blow up. Things would get better for a while. We would make plans, we would pretend to be happy, and then without notice something would set him off and the cycle would start again.

I was standing at the washing machine doing laundry when I realized that the girls and I would be better off divorced than living a life based on lies. I didn't know where that thought came from or what it meant, but I knew, at that moment, I had options. I didn't have to keep living like that. The thoughts in my head that had tried to convince me that this type of love was better than not being loved at all were lies. I knew that I didn't have to be treated that way anymore and that it wasn't love.

Revealing the truth was much more difficult than I anticipated. My husband's threats and violence seemed more than I could possibly handle. He kicked us out of our home, he drained the bank accounts, he kidnapped the girls, and he took me through an incredibly expensive court battle. He was determined to destroy me. I was determined not to let him destroy me or my girls.

I was twenty-one years old. I was divorced, was awarded sole custody of my two daughters, and was now on my own. We were penniless. What was I going to do to support my little women? The only education I had was based on what I had learned from being involved in sports. So I went to work coaching swimming and began developing a small business called C.A.S.H. Sports. The company hosted volleyball and basketball leagues and tournaments for corporations. C.A.S.H. Sports grew to include a clothing line and a youth division, combining sports and character education. I started C.A.S.H. Sports as a way to pay for our lives, but the name represented what was really important to me:

C: Carlette

A: Amanda

S: Sara

H: Hower (our last name)

It was our family business!

I was twenty-nine years old. Steve Patterson became a client of C.A.S.H. Sports, and we began working together on sports ventures.

I started to notice a theme evolving in my life. My life was about love.

My love for swimming introduced me to the world of sports. My love of volleyball and basketball gave me the foundation to start a company, a company that eventually led me to meet a man that gave me love. My love for playing dolls prepared me for the best part of my life, being a mom. My love for my little women gave me the courage and the strength to stand up for myself and create a life based on love and truth. When my Granddaddy Lewis died, I learned that love hurts. My Grandmother Lewis's unconditional love for me showed me what God's love for me was like, and I was able to live a life based on faith because of that love.

I began to see the power of God's love in my life. He had let me make my own choices, do things my way, go for all the things life screamed at me to get. He watched me, his child, struggle, cry, and beg for something different. Yet he could not change the choices I had made.

Going through a divorce, being a single mom, raising two fabulous little women, running a business — these were all my choices. Listening to my ex-husband's promises of riches and fame taught me a tough lesson. I had sold my soul to my ex-husband, but God never left me, He never stopped loving me, and the minute I asked for his help, he was there for me. He was so excited to show me all that he had planned for me and how to do it his way, not mine. To him be the glory!

CHAPTER TWO
Faith

Most of the time, throughout my life, I thought I knew what I was doing and felt that I was in charge of my life. Those words alone give you a glimpse into how little faith I lived by.

My first understanding of faith was based on what I learned as a child growing up in a wonderful Christian home. My second understanding of faith was what I relied on as an adult when life was challenging. My third understanding of faith was begging God for answers. Today I understand faith as the simple comfort of knowing that God has an amazing life planned for me. I may not be able to see all the details, but I know in my heart that he has each one planned out better than I could ever imagine.

My faith is not always strong. My actions are not always worthy. My words are not always gentle. My life has been messy, but that's how I've learned about faith.

I began to find depth in the word *faith* when I ran out of ways to make my life work. It was during the quiet nights when I felt the loneliness of being alone. It was when I was faced with powerful questions and didn't want to recite the usual answers anymore. It was when my heart finally took over and my head and ego got out of the way. I touched faith. I wanted more.

As I played the story of my life back in my head, the only drive that I saw was toward dreams that other people had for me, nothing that I would call my own. No wonder life seemed so empty. Here I was spending all my time trying to impress or please others.

Why had I given up on my dreams? The feeling of anticipation and excitement was a distant memory, so blurry that I couldn't even remotely make out what it looked like. How, why, and when did that happen?

How was it that simple moments, staggered throughout days and years, came to define me and my life? I now know that each person that I considered a "bump" was a bump into faith. I needed that person to bump me into my next moment, which led me to my next leap of faith.

I thought about all the jobs I had taken that took me so far away from my heart. I replayed words I had said and things I had done that didn't sound remotely like who I wanted to be. Time began to tell a story in which I no longer played the main character, and it was a story I wasn't proud to play any character in.

Only in the quiet moments of reflection was I able to see how simple it was to take the steps that led me away from me. I had chosen what I thought was the easiest road, and it had led me to the hardest journey. I didn't know exactly what to do, but I felt compelled to do something different.

During the brief moments when I was raw and available to God's love, I noticed my life beginning to change. I saw something that reminded me of something I used to love. I tasted flavors I had forgotten. I felt safe. I heard sounds of nature that had been drowned out by my life's noise. The world began to look different. It felt different. It sounded different. And then my heart began to beat in a way that was a faint memory. I liked the naked pounding. It felt familiar. It was powerful. It was perfect.

God's love is the only compass we need to find our way back to ourselves. He sent us here. He gave us everything we need for our journey. He loves us. He guides us. He blesses us. And he is available to us whenever we need him. For that, I give thanks. I call all these beliefs *faith*.

CHAPTER THREE
Amanda's Story

Amanda is my oldest daughter. She's always been a bit different than other kids. She didn't fit in at school, and she didn't have any friends. Most everyone was mean to her and made fun of the way she looked, talked, and acted. Sara and I were her only friends. We pretended that it was okay, but it was a heavy burden, always covering up for the way Amanda acted. Amanda knew in her heart that she was different, but Sara and I didn't want her to be different; we wanted her to be normal, so she tried everything she could to be that for us.

As a mom, different can be a heartbreaker when it's in reference to your child. Amanda was a year-and-a-half old when we decided to search for answers why she wasn't developing like other children. Doctors did extensive blood work and testing but were not able to figure out a diagnosis. What they did know was that she wasn't developing as a normal child should and there was reason for concern. They told us that based on her test results, they didn't expect her to walk or talk or lead a normal life. Life changed after that doctor's appointment.

I was nineteen years old, seven months pregnant, and my husband was twenty-seven years old the day we had that doctor's appointment. At first we were determined to prove that the doctors and the test results were wrong. But as time went on, Amanda continued to miss developmental milestones.

We owned health clubs for a living and were doing very well. Just a year and a half earlier, we had brought Amanda home from the hospital in a Rolls Royce. My husband said over and over that his kids would never want for anything and that he would take care of us all for the rest of our lives. Well, that proved much more difficult to do with the news that life wasn't going to unfold the way we had planned. He began traveling more and more, staying away longer and longer, and didn't make it home for Sara's birth.

I knew that God didn't make mistakes, and I knew that nothing about Amanda was a mistake. She was his amazing, beautiful daughter, and he had great plans for her life. Day by day, Amanda, Sara, and I grew up together without my husband. When I would put Sara down for a nap, Amanda and I would swim together in our pool. I would strap her on my back and swim laps, her little legs just kicking away. We spent our afternoons reading books and working through the simple task of saying words and trying to make Amanda's body do what came so easily for other toddlers.

Through God's amazing grace and love, Amanda began to walk and talk and giggle and do all the other things that little children do — just in her own time and in her own way. Every day, I gave praise for God's blessings on my little woman. I knew she was a gift and that she had so much to teach me. I started trying to figure out the world that she lived in rather than forcing her to live in mine. Both our worlds had good and bad, so together, we figured out how to create a life filled with as much good from both our worlds as we could squeeze into a day.

It hurt to watch Amanda be different. But mainly it hurt my ego that she wasn't like everyone else's kids. Lesson number one: God wants his children to be who he created them to be, not what the world tries to convince us they should be. It was a tough lesson to embrace, but I wrapped myself in his love.

That was how I coped with Amanda being different; I turned to God to show me how. As I was turning to God, my husband was turning to everything but God. Our worlds were drifting apart. My husband and I had very different beliefs about God and faith long before Amanda. When life got tough, the facades that we hid behind crumbled, and we were left exposed. Amanda gave us this gift of purity. Both my husband and I had lived a life based on winning, and God was going to show us how to win for his glory rather than ours. He gave us Amanda as our teacher.

I was so fascinated by all that I was learning from my very young teacher, Amanda, that I wrote an article for Christian Family magazine. At a young age, Amanda already had a message for the world, and God chose me to be her writer.

Let's Play Life
Written in 1983 when Amanda was four months old.

"Attention, Mr. and Mrs. Hower! Your life has just come to an abrupt halt. You have just given birth to an 8-pound, 13 ½ ounce bundle of responsibility." A doctor of reality would proclaim such an explanation after delivery; instead, the doctors of today kindly state the child's sex and leave the rest up to you.

Welcome to the world of baby babbling, bottles, and little buns. Our relationship did not begin with a big hug or a formal introduction. Much to my dismay, I was handed a petite creature that fell asleep after her first glance of me.

I stared at her in disbelief. This is it! I thought to myself. She seemed twice that size when she was lodged between my ribs and four times that size when she was making her debut. So these are the tiny little feet that tap-danced nightly. My, how they seem to have calmed down. So this is childbirth. . .

The cover was off the box, and the game of life was underway. I began explaining the rules of the game to Amanda and exactly how I expected her to play. Well, Amanda knew from the beginning that she was her own player and she rolled her own dice. Tucked away tightly in her blankets, she created her own rules for her game of life.

After many weeks of total chaos and no sleep, I realized, as a parent, that at this rate Amanda and I were not going to finish the game successfully. I knew I could not continue such an important game in a boggled state of mind, so I set out in search of the sanity cards. Lo and behold, I found Amanda holding the cards labeled "Life in a Child's World."

From Amanda, I drew my first card, labeled "Joy." Joy, to me, was sleeping until noon, having chocolate for lunch, and spending the evening with a good book. This definition was nowhere to be found in Amanda's card labeled "Joy." Joy, to her, meant waking up before the sun, playing life all day, and trying to sleep through as little darkness as possible. Amanda moved ahead two spaces, and I was sent back for another card.

From Amanda's deck, I drew the card labeled "Faith." My definition: if things are not going my way, do whatever it takes to change their direction. Her definition: complete trust. She knew absolutely nothing of this game of life, yet she never doubted the moves I commanded her to take. Once again she moved ahead in the game, and I was sent back to try again.

My next card read "Inspiration." My definition: Amanda! Every day I watched her struggle with different tasks, yet every day I watched her determination grow to fulfill her desires. She taught me life without limitations, as she knew of none, and she always found a way to accomplish just what she set out to do. After reading this card, I was sent back to "Go" to watch Amanda finish the game as she wished the rules to be played.

I watched her cry out in pain as life taught her lessons, and I watched her learn and accept instead of lashing out in anger. I watched her feel pain; I watched her accept comfort. She taught me communication without ever saying a word. She gave me love without ever knowing of its existence. I now play by Amanda's rules and have grown to love life without time. She has taught me how the game of life should be played.

As Amanda and I embrace each new day with curious minds and open hearts, we learn the joys of life. Many days pass with little change, but I have learned from Amanda that each tomorrow brings yesterday's discoveries, today's adventures, and tomorrow's dreams all into focus. Amanda not only takes the time to smell the roses, fortunately, she eats them too!

As good as things were with Amanda, they were that bad with my husband. He had given his life over to drugs and was abusive whenever he showed up at home. We battled it out in court for years, and finally our marriage was over. When I was awarded sole custody of the girls, he was so furious at me that he said he would never pay me a dime or see the girls again.

It was so sad to watch so many lives being changed. It was ugly. It was bitter. It was sin at its worst, and our lives were being ripped apart daily. But, we had each other, and my now ex-husband went on to have a different life for himself, without us.

CHAPTER FOUR
Sara's Story

Amanda and Sara were twenty months apart. Sara loved every aspect of life. She walked and talked at nine months; it was as if she had so much to do and say that she couldn't get started fast enough. She was fine with our little life of mom and her little women, until she went to school. That's where she started to figure out that our family was different. She didn't want our family to be different. She didn't want a sister that the other kids made fun of; it broke her heart. She wanted a daddy like the other kids had. She wanted a mom that didn't work all the time. She wanted to buy nice clothes from the mall, not wear the sportswear that her mom had created. She wanted a life that was nothing like the one she had. I knew that, and it was an awful feeling to know that I couldn't give her the things she wanted.

Sara had such a tender heart. She felt the pain of the world, but her young mind and soul just couldn't figure out how to make everything better. She tried to be happy. She tried to be a good child for me. She tried to make me happy. But she was sad.

She lived with a hole in her heart and soul because she couldn't figure out why her daddy didn't want her. Her child brain couldn't make sense of what she had done that was so bad that her own daddy wouldn't want to be around her. She couldn't make sense of why he didn't even want to see her.

During the day, Sara put up a great front of being happy and okay with life — but at night, she cried. She hurt. As she grew up, her pain and confusion grew with her. Love is such a powerful desire; if she couldn't get it from her daddy, she would find it somewhere else, and so began her search for someone or something to fill the void.

As a young, single mom, I just tried to survive. I prayed I'd be able to pay our rent every month, that I could cover the girls' school tuition and health bills, and that I could buy them what was necessary to make them feel normal. Month after month, and year after year, we did it! Thank you, Jesus!

My focus was on the big things, and I missed the little things. I missed that Sara was lonely. I didn't know the burden I placed on her to always make sure Amanda was okay. When she shared her heart with me, I would glaze over it with a song or a prayer, but I don't think she ever felt like I really listened to her. I probably didn't, because if I heard what she said, it would break my heart. I knew I wasn't able to give her the life she wanted, but instead of facing it, I just worked harder to try to buy it for her.

We all hurt inside, but we covered it up because we didn't want one another to know how sad we were. During the day, we all wore our happy faces and tried to do what made everyone else happy or pleased with us, in hopes that we would be liked and accepted. We were growing up together, the three of us.

CHAPTER FIVE
When Does Forever Begin?

I was twenty-nine years old when I scheduled a meeting with Steve Patterson, the executive director of Grand Canyon State Games. As president of C.A.S.H. Sports, I thought our businesses had enough similarities that we should meet to talk about collaboration. It was an early morning meeting, and I had raced through the morning ritual of getting my little women off to school so I would be on time for the meeting. I arrived a bit early and waited in the lobby for Steve. After twenty minutes, his assistant said he was sorry but Steve was not going to be able to make our meeting and could we reschedule. I left disappointed and wondering if it was even worth rescheduling.

Weeks passed, and as our schedules finally permitted, we set up another meeting. The timing was good for both of us. Steve was looking for someone to develop and launch the Corporate Games and I was looking for new clients. Steve's staff meetings were on Wednesdays, so that was my one day working for him. The work he wanted me to do on that one day required two or three days' work. Steve wanted excellence in every detail. The feeling that nothing I did was good enough for him got old, and soon he was not one of my favorite clients. I began to dread Wednesdays.

I was known for leaving an inspirational quote on my business answering machine. I had books of quotes, and Coach John Wooden was my all-time favorite. Every day, I read through them and found the one that I wanted to share with whoever called me but instead got my answering machine. One day when I chose a quote from Coach Wooden, Steve called. When I returned his call, he shared with me that he had played basketball at UCLA for Coach Wooden. That explained Steve's attention to detail and his expectation for excellence. I shared with him that Coach Wooden was one of my favorite people and that I modeled my life and my business after his teachings. This was the first somewhat personal conversation Steve and I ever had. It was simple. It was short, but we understood each other in a different way after that. Wednesdays became my Wooden Days on my answering machine. Steve and I settled into respecting each other's desire to do our best when our best was needed — one of Coach's sayings.

Just as Steve had hoped, our hard work paid off and we were both pleased with the inaugural year of the Corporate Games. We went on to work together for a couple more years on different projects. As a single mom, I worked hard but never spent any extra time socializing with my clients. Instead, as soon as my work was done, I wanted to get home to my little women. Steve knew this about me because Amanda and Sara accompanied me to our meetings when I had to work late or on the weekends. As Steve and I mapped out our latest business projects, we never shared personal stories or spent time getting to know each other's history. We spent hours working side by side but remained distant.

The years were passing by. My little women were ten and eleven years old. We were strong for each other, but each of us longed to be loved. No matter how much I tried to convince myself and my little women that we were fine, just the three of us, our hearts wanted so much more. This "more" that we wanted was not something we talked about; it was a deep feeling that we kept tucked away. If we had talked about it, then we would have had to acknowledge that we wanted more than what we had.

Almost without notice, the obligations of each day were beginning to crowd out the passions of my heart. I'm not sure when the soul-felt desire to spend forever with someone that I loved began to disappear. What I did notice was that year after year when I sat down in front of a warm December fire to write my birthday wishes, they were more about being able to meet my responsibilities than meeting someone to share my life with.

When I wasn't too tired from the tasks of the day, I would talk to God about what he wanted for my life. I knew he loved me; I could feel his love. I believed and hoped that his plans for my life included love, joy, abundance, grace, and passion, just to mention a few. Unfortunately, the world I lived in, day in and day out, seemed totally disconnected from the tender, safe embrace of a God that was paying attention to the reality of my life.

Maybe I had it all wrong, I decided. Maybe the love that I longed for was not possible. Maybe I needed to let go of wanting forever with the love of my life.

CHAPTER SIX
C

I was working late, preparing for a business trip I was taking the next day. As I was leaving the office, arms filled with more work than I could possibly get done before takeoff the next day, Steve handed me a large envelope. I wasn't happy about that. I thought, *how could he possibly be giving me more work to get done?*

Driving home, I decided to open the envelope as I waited in traffic. *C*, it was hand written. This was different; Steve had always been formal with me. As I began to read, I became lost in the passionate words that filled the pages. Never before had I read such tender thoughts, such emotion expressed in words.

Who wrote this? I had to pull over, stop my car, and skip to the last page to see who signed it. I had never read such poetry, such an expression of love, such tenderness, such compassion for parts of me I thought no one even knew. That moment became frozen in time for me. I can tell you the sounds of the traffic, the heat of the day beating into my car, the overwhelmed and tired feelings I felt in my heart, the pulse of the moment when I felt that I was holding love.

It's hard to explain what words on a page can do to your heart, but I can truly say those words, those thoughts he had taken the time to share with me, taking a chance and revealing himself to me — they were the gift of a lifetime.

When I arrived home, I put the letter back in its envelope and transitioned back into being a mom. It was time for dinner, and my little women would be waiting for something good to eat. Steve called. "Carlette, how are you?"

"Oh, fine thank you."

"I just wanted to make sure you were okay, that I didn't offend you or anything. You know you don't have to respond at all; I just needed you to know how I feel about you."

"Okay, wow, your writing is so beautiful. Thank you."

"Talk to you later."

"Goodbye."

We hung up. I cooked dinner. I packed. I never stopped thinking about the words that Steve had written to me. They were foreign to me. No one had ever said the things that he said to me, much less someone that I had never shared my personal story with. I was confused. Was it even possible that Steve Patterson, a man I had worked with for years, had powerful feelings toward me?

I got on the plane and reread every word written in the letter, over and over and over. I arrived at my hotel, and dozens of roses were waiting in my room. Every woman's dream, all playing out for me thanks to a man I had known for years — but I obviously knew nothing about him. Nor had I really cared to know anything personal about him; he was just a client, a tough client at that.

After unpacking and rereading the letter, I called him. No answer, so I left a message, thanking him for the roses. Days passed. I worked, and he didn't call back. To say that my mind was racing in a million different directions would be an understatement. I was beginning to wonder if any of it was real. All I knew was that I was different because of what he wrote to me. What I didn't know was that him having the courage to tell me how he felt about me was going to be the beginning of a new life for me and my little women.

These are the words that changed my world forever ...

C

I hope you're having a good day. I want to thank you for making many of my days good and happy ones by your bright smile and cheerful, kind words to me.

There is so much I want to say to you that cannot or has not been said; because of time, or convention, or...but I believe that the <u>word</u>, be it spoken or written, is what makes us human. In an effort to speak, a need to speak, to communicate my thoughts, my feelings, my plans, my dreams, my fears, my love ... I take paper to pen, to make the abstract real. This is how we as humans create ... we speak, we communicate, we define our reality and in so doing we invent possibility.

"In the beginning was the <u>Word</u>"... "God <u>said</u>, let there be light." In language and speaking, we have been given the power of God. I do not speak lightly or without deep consideration. I speak because I must. I cannot do otherwise.

I do not wish to burden you or control you but merely to speak of me and you and what you are coming to mean to me. If it serves no other purpose than to fulfill my desire to have you know me better and to touch you in some fundamental way, then I am satisfied.

I have not been actively searching for you, but you have entered my life. You have stirred some deep emotional well that has been capped for many, many, years. What is it? What the _hell_ is it? It is certainly not nothing. I am grateful. I am alive. I am entranced. . .by you, by me, by life, by the future, by opportunity to grow, to evolve, to begin, to share, to support, to touch, to feel, to laugh, to cry, to work, to live in a new and happy way. What about you?

I admire your independence and wonder at your strength to carry the burden of lives that you do with style and spirit. Do you ever despair? Do you long for help and companionship and strength when times grow tough? You seem undaunted. Is it your act? Are you for real? You smile and shrug and make my arms and my heart ache. I long to hold you and lift you and add my two cents to your dollar.

I long to hear your story. I could ask you a million questions and still want to hear more.

Likewise, I want to share a part of me that approaches all of me with someone who I really hardly know. Why? What is it that I see in you that draws me? That makes me believe that what I am, and what I say or do matters to you, that I fulfill a longing or a space in your universe? I just sense it. I believe it. I know it. Do you?

I seek new vistas. . .to walk and talk and laugh and love in spring rain. I complete a journey, and stand at the edge of the continent. I hear the ocean breakers roar and taste the salt air, feel the sun beating on my raw skin. I am renewed, I am refreshed, and I scan the horizon for my path forward. May I take your hand? May I look in your eyes? May I walk the beach with you? May our footprints dance along the waterline? Do I dare? Do you dare?

Digressions: I have long been a solitary creature. I am surrounded by people, friends, family…but in most ways alone. I read, I meditate, I wish, I pray, I live, I provide, I lead. . .but rarely do I share me. . .what's inside. It seems okay to me. I observe the male patterns in the animal kingdom and see the solitary males, who mate, who raise their young then wander off to the siren of some inner voice. Is that me? Can it be otherwise?

I _know_ my work here and now is nearly done. What lies ahead? I have given it little thought. Have had little time to give it thought. I have little cared to give it thought, and here *you* come. Or maybe it's just really me. Its readiness, its longing. That is what I wonder.

I have long believed, but little spoke of true love and passion and meaning in relationship. I gave it up with the bloom of youth for the hard reality of obligation and commitment. I have no regrets. I am proud of my work, my life, my family. I have achieved much in an area where many fail, or fail to try. I have the peace that comes from having given your best whatever the outcome. (Sounds like John Wooden!)

> *In which direction do you travel?*
> *How do *you* choose the tune?*
> *Is there room for another?*
> *Or is it, simply, just too soon*
> *To what greater rhythms do you ramble?*
> *Through what branches do your winds blow?*
> *How does your spirit rise?*
> *As through this life you go*
> *I am a nearby presence*
> *Drawn by the radiation of your sun*
> *Seeking, hoping, praying, longing*
> *To be with you as one.*
> *S*

I finished my business trip, packed my bags, and flew back to Phoenix. When I arrived home, it was in the middle of a business day, and I had a standing, weekly meeting with Steve on that day. Very nervous and totally raw emotionally, I went to the meeting—not sure of anything at that point. Due to my plane being late, I arrived after the meeting had started; we had a team of people meeting with us about our project. I slipped into the meeting and sat down in the empty chair next to Steve. The meeting followed the agenda, and when my time to report came up, I shared my work. At the end of the meeting, as everyone was leaving, Steve handed me another envelope. We had back-to-back meetings scheduled, so we didn't exchange any other words with each other.

Meeting after meeting dragged by until finally the end of the day arrived. It would be on the drive home, again, that I would get to know him a bit more, based on what he had chosen to write to me while I was away.

C

How do I begin to approach you? To build a trust that will not fail? How do I begin to reach you? Against what odds must I prevail?

What hidden trials and tempests beset you? How can I calm your storm-tossed seas? How can I soothe the beast within you? When will you cease to flee?

I long to hold the child within you. To build a trust that will <u>not</u> fail. To take your hand and walk beside you. To that end I will prevail.

God's gift of grace and beauty has been abundantly bestowed upon you. Why have you spent it so carelessly? To what selfish demands of others have you succumbed? Others have not earned your love and respect. You travel with the baggage of abuse and neglect and misuse. My anger swells up in my throat and I fight to contain it. <u>Look at me!</u>

You smile and laugh. You carry on! You love your little women with a passion and a glory that honors the purity of your soul. Your soul that remains unloved and unbroken. Your soul that calls to me. That seeks me without fully knowing. Like heavenly bodies held in orbit. We are drawn and held…attracted by the sum of our yearning for unity and peace and purpose and joy!

Oh rare commodity. The peace of God and the love of another! They are inseparable. Only as we know Him, our creator, can we know ourselves and what we are meant to be. Love can surely be understood and experienced in the context of His love for us and the grace and forgiveness of the divine for creation…or mother and daughter…that can conquer <u>all</u>.

I cannot fully describe and cannot fully share the depths of my awaking love for you. It is without reason or logic. By nature of time and sharing, still incomplete. You cannot deny it. Is it right for you? Have you been dashed once too many times to take a chance? Am I for real?

Over the past ten plus years in this community I have labored for the respect and position that can frame a life's work. It is far from finished, but a firm foundation has been laid.

In my early thirties, about your age, I had squandered prodigious gifts of talents, brains, support and respect with selfish, tempered pleasure and childish indulgence. I reached a bottom and with God's help I have arrived at the moment that you see me today. I know how precious it is and how quickly it can be destroyed with self-indulgence and carelessness.

What I have gained is strength of patience, and constancy and endurance that only time and devoted labor can achieve. There is a quality that commitment can bring to a man and a relationship. I believe that I have been called and led by the unseen hand of almighty to salvage the best of what might have been. To Him be the glory!

I wish you could know my boys. They are becoming young men I am very proud of. They are part of my ultimate legacy with much more to come.

What I seek now is to begin to peel away the layers of scar tissue that cover your heart. To allow you the opportunity to trust another as today you only trust yourself.

There is nothing that is hidden from me. I do not know your specifics (although I long to) yet I know the generalities enough to assure you that you need hide <u>nothing</u> from me. No past history, or action or cause or effect. All form a part of the fabric that we can weave together if we will it. I will it.

<u>Nothing</u> can separate you from my love for you. Not time, or distance, or work or deed. I am devoted to your happiness and prosperity and the future of your little ones. Please make any request that you wish and test my devotion to you.

I have missed my daily <u>C</u> fix. Welcome back. I embrace you.
S

CHAPTER SEVEN
Love

It wasn't until something so unexpected, so unplanned by me and so perfectly written entered into my world that I was introduced to a different level of love. I had felt love as a mother, and I was loved by my family. The love that was missing from my life was a passionate, adult love.

There are many different kinds of love, and I wanted a passionate love that connected to my soul, that went beyond the thrill of dating or the encounter of sex. As much as I had faith that I would find love, and hope that I would be loved, the love that I was handed was more complicated and deeper than anything I had ever known.

I didn't know when Steve began to love me. I didn't know the circumstances that he was living in or anything at all about his past. I didn't know the obligations that he felt in his heart or the promises he made to himself. I only knew what he chose to tell me.

My days consisted of working, raising a family, and striving to meet all the obligations and responsibilities that life gave me. I was not bitter or hopeless, just busy doing what was expected of me. There was not much me left in my life, except for the quiet nights I spent alone, writing, dreaming, and hoping that someday I would meet someone who wanted what I had to offer.

The moment Steve handed me those letters, I began the journey of healing. Healing from a life of neglect. I had been the one who had neglected myself. I was the one who didn't love me. I was the person who was causing all of my pain.

When Steve handed me his heart, I did not know exactly what to do with it, but I didn't question his motives, his words, or his intentions. I accepted his love because I wanted to be loved. I struggled with his love because I was afraid of being loved. I learned to love because I let him love me, faults and all. I now have an abundance of love because I accepted his love.

Through the experience of being loved, I now know that love is a gift, not to be treasured all alone. From the depth of my soul, I believe that love can only become what it is destined to be if we are willing to read its tender words, written in unfamiliar places — add our story to its pages and pass it along to someone else.

CHAPTER EIGHT
Frozen Pizza and Wine

Our first date was Steve bringing over a frozen pizza and a great bottle of wine after I put my little women to bed. As I stood in my kitchen, watching Steve unpack a grocery bag, opening a box of pizza, and asking for a couple of wine glasses, I thought, *Who is this guy? What the heck am I doing with him in my kitchen?*

Where did we possibly begin? We knew so much about each other professionally, but personally, we knew nothing. I am sad to say, I had never even cared to know anything about Steve personally. Oh, I knew he had a couple of boys; we would always ask how the kids were doing in passing, but that was it — nothing remotely deep enough for him to write me such amazing love letters.

I was nervous to do or say anything because I didn't want him to rethink everything he had written once he got to know me. When he began to hear the chapters of my life story, would he run like hell and retract every passionate word he had written? It was beyond scary, but it was so romantic that I have to say, he had me at *C*.

One of the first things Steve discovered about me was that I didn't have any wine glasses. I didn't drink. Steve, on the other hand, was a wine connoisseur. So, we poured our first glass of wine together into a couple of plastic cups, enjoyed our frozen pizza, and began to get to know each other.

Everything about that night was perfect. I found myself looking at Steve, listening to him and his stories and thinking, *wow, what the heck is happening here?* Night after night, Steve brought me dinner after I put my little women to bed. And night after night, we shared our stories.

Slowly we were letting go of our past and moving into a future — together. It was the simple sips of wine and cool evenings enjoying the backyard beauty that began to write our new chapters together. Steve knew best how to describe what we were feeling. This is a poem he wrote for me…

For Carlette —
Thou art the sky on a midsummer's night
With dry, limpid breezes and soft purple light
Stars flutter by without seeming
While you bring sweet kisses for raspberry dreaming.

To measure thy presence in earth time and space
Is hopeless a task as through life we race
Yet raspberry dreaming in soft twilight glow
Brings laughter and pleasure that only we know.

With our arms we embrace the love of the ages
As each day we inscribe our lives on its pages
Thine heart to me given without question of favor
Is the sweet gift of life with raspberry flavor.

Steve

CHAPTER NINE
Surviving Life

As much as Amanda, Sara, and I all tried to hide our pain, Steve saw it. He wrote about it in his letters to me. It was like he could see my soul. He could feel the pain I felt as a mother, not able to provide for my children. He wanted to give me and my little women everything we ever wanted. He wanted to be the daddy that my girls longed to have. He wanted to show us what it meant to feel love, to live love, to have a life that included a mom and a dad, to be a family — what we all wanted.

As beautiful as our love story began, living through it wasn't so easy. Our children and the people we worked for were not pleased with our relationship. It was as if they were all determined to tear us apart. And one by one, they took their toll on us.

Steve and I dated for a couple of years. As I was falling in love with him, Sara felt like I was falling out of love with her. She felt like Steve was taking me away from her. She had already lost one parent and didn't want to lose another one. This was a silent battle that began; I had no idea what was happening. We didn't talk about it. It just grew into big, ugly feelings. It was so confusing for Sara because Steve was offering her everything she wanted, but her heart and her mind couldn't comprehend how it could possibly be happening. She didn't have any memory of her dad being nice to her or loving her, so the more Steve tried to love her, the more she rejected him. She was afraid he would leave her too, and she already knew how much that hurt. Her goal was to protect herself because now her mom wasn't even on her side anymore. Steve and I grew closer, and Sara and I began to grow apart.

Instead of relying on our family to feel love, Sara began seeking love from anything else that could help her not to feel sad. She thought if she cut her hair, she would be loved. If she acted a certain way, if she had certain friends, wore expensive clothes, the list went on and on. Steve and I tried to give her everything on her list. The more we gave, the more she wanted and needed, but nothing satisfied her. None of us could figure out how to make Sara happy. It was sad to watch such a beautiful soul become so mad at the world. She was just a little kid with a great big heart that wanted to be loved, but she didn't know how to ask for it or receive it.

Our courtship began to feel more like a merger or a hostile takeover, depending on who you asked. Steve and I both had lives that were being disrupted because we wanted to be together. No one knew our story. No one knew the tender words that left Steve's heart and found permanence on the pages of the love letters he handed to me. Nor did Steve and I want to share any part of our raw, new love. We wanted to protect it because it felt so deep. It was something we had both longed for, and now that we finally had it, we didn't want anyone to take it away from us. We weren't loving each other to hurt anyone; we were loving each other because something about who we were, the lives we had led and the lives that lay before us, needed each other to write the rest of our story.

Day by day, month by month, our worlds began to unravel. At work, we were accused of a long-time love affair. Not true. We both had very different, separate lives until the day the love letters exchanged hands. No matter what lies others wanted to declare, we knew the truth.

It seems quite naive as I write about it now, but at that point in our lives, we both believed that the truth always wins. Steve and I wanted to do the right thing for ourselves, for our families, and for our work. It was a deep desire that served as our compass as we navigated through life. We wanted to be able to take care of our families and for them to know how much we loved them. We wanted to be able to do great work in our communities. And now we wanted to share it all with each other. This simple desire brought about sadness and heartache as we faced the truth of what changes we would be required to make if we wanted to be together.

As Steve and I tried to maneuver through personal and professional changes, our hearts were changing, but we were not sure how or what to do with all the changes to make everyone happy. This was one of our first mistakes, thinking we could make everyone happy. Instead, we pleased no one, including ourselves. We seemed to get lost in trying to be all things to all people, and in no time, we had lost our way. We were living out other people's story and had decided that ours was not important. Instead of taking some time to sort through the chaos, we just tried our best to manage the problem of the moment. We both did a poor job of managing these changes and the people they affected. It absolutely was not our intention, but looking back, I wish we could have do-overs. At the same time, it's hard to say where I would start with those do-overs, because for every choice we made, we were blessed with a layer of life that brought depth and understanding as we began to build our lives together.

Neither one of us would have chosen a do-over with our first marriages because we both received the precious gifts of our children. Those children challenged us to become the man and woman we became because we wanted so much for them. Our first marriages were filled with gifts and blessings. Steve and I both regretted many things from our first marriages, but we made peace with the fact that we did the best we could at that time in our lives. The pain that divorce causes for everyone involved is a deep scar that never goes away. It's a scar that reminds us of our choices and our consequences. Every day we live with that scar, knowing there's nothing we can do to change it. We thank God for the gift of forgiveness, because without it, we would not be able to heal and move forward with the life he has planned for us.

We both would have loved do-overs in our careers because we wanted so much to serve our communities and we messed that up. I was passionate about changing the world and I was adamant about people doing the right thing. I wanted to make a difference, and I had so many ideas about how to make that happen. I wasn't smooth in my delivery though. I wasn't educated in the politics of organizations, and I let my passion take over when I wanted to get something done. Over and over, I was told I needed to change, but I wasn't sure how to do that while still maintaining my passion and deep desire to make a difference.

During my journey of trying to change to fit in with what society wanted, a turning point took place as I stood in the lobby of a New York hotel. A group of us were there working, and I had a moment with the chairman of the board while we were waiting for the others to arrive. I began sharing my passion for a project with him, and after listening to me, he said, "Carlette, when you're getting raped, instead of fighting it, you need to learn to lie back and enjoy it." I have never forgotten those words. How could the chairman of our board, an older man that I was supposed to look up to and respect, say something so damaging?

It was that type of thinking that Steve and I wanted to change. Was there a way to do meaningful work that was aligned with our hearts and the hearts of organizations in our community? We were holding on to our desire to be agents of change, but we had no idea how tough this mission was going to get. As our professional careers continued, so did our tough lessons.

Through it all, Steve and I were learning a different kind of love than either one of us had ever experienced. We knew that love involved pain because as parents, we felt so much love for our children that when they hurt or when we could not make it all better for them, we felt a pain that touched the core of our being. We were okay with pain.

We felt connected, as if we needed each other to make the rest of our lives make sense. We were unsure about what to do with these feelings because they made us feel vulnerable. The reality of change was a huge risk, and we could lose everything we had worked so hard to have. Our hearts knew how lonely a life of working just to please others was, and the depth of the connection we felt made us willing to take risks.

We wanted to be together. We had prayed for a relationship like ours. Love had come to mean sharing each other — the good, the bad, the ugly, the unsure, the unknown. That love gave us the courage to commit our lives to each other. To honor and cherish each other until death do us part. We packed up all the kids, called our families, and boarded a plane for Hawaii. We celebrated our commitment to each other by getting married on Makena Beach in Maui.

Within a couple of years, we had gone from having great careers, financial stability, and happy children to losing everything and starting over, all because we loved each other.

It was Christmas Eve, and Steve and I were at the office. We had been working for another large sports organization for a couple years. The board had approved us working together as a married couple. Steve was the CEO, and I was a vice president. It was early in the afternoon when Steve received a call from the chairman of the board. The board thought we were too strong as a couple, so I had to go; they wanted him to fire me that day. The cause was that I was his wife. What a horrible situation to put Steve in. He spent hours trying to find a different solution, but their minds were made up.

He walked out of his office and into mine. He looked awful. He told me what he had been asked to do and handed me a business card of an attorney, Loral Deatherage. I packed up my belongings and was escorted out of the building. To say a tough holiday followed would be an understatement!

Things were not only tough professionally, personally they were awful too. Oh the misery of a blended family. We had broken our children's hearts by loving each other. One by one, they demonstrated their anger, their pain, their frustration, and their brokenness. We tried everything to somehow bring love back into their lives, but we failed.

Steve's sons were in college, and we spent very little time with them. Steve longed to share his life with them and missed the simple joys of hearing from them. What once was a strong bond between father and sons was now shattered into a million broken pieces, and none of us knew how to put the pieces together again.

Amanda and Sara were struggling through their teenage years, and no matter what we tried to do, it was the wrong thing and they never missed a moment to let us know how miserable we made them. As if we had not already ruined their lives enough, Steve and I had a baby, Makena. There was a fifteen-year difference between her and Sara.

It was time for a new beginning. We needed to figure out how to take all that we had learned and do something good with it. Steve and I loved working together; we were a good team. We decided we would start our own company, Patterson Sports Ventures, and our mission was to be Agents of Change. Together we would commit our time and resources to causes we believed in and enjoy the journey of raising another child together.

As we lived through the ups and downs of life, we began to understand the depth of love. Every word that Steve had written to me many years earlier had been tested beyond any level of passion or commitment we could have dreamed possible.

Love is an overwhelming desire that penetrates our intellect and lives within our hearts. I now know that something much bigger than Steve drove him to take pen to paper and reveal the depth of his heart to me.

CHAPTER TEN
Our Summer Project

It was the summer of 2004. All of our children were off at college, and Steve and I had only Makena, now five years old, living with us. It was time to remodel our home as well as our lives. A couple of years earlier, we had started talking about all the changes we wanted to make. We spent our evenings, wine in hand, designing our new life and home. We wished that we lived in Monterey, California, but because work and family were in Phoenix, we decided to build a beach house in the desert.

This was going to be our summer project — yes, we were going to do it ourselves. Steve had experience being a general contractor in his earlier years, and it was something we could do together. We had packed up all of our belongings, and they were in a storage unit in our front yard. Oh the fun of construction. We were living out of the back bedrooms, existing with a very basic kitchen, and spending most of our time in work clothes. Sara and Makena were part of our work crew, and together as a family, we were remodeling our home and rebuilding our lives.

The walls and the ceilings had been torn down. Wires hung exposed, and duct tape kept them and us out of danger. The carpet had been removed, and the rough concrete was left exposed. Tiled floor had been jack hammered up, leaving only dirt. Windows were boarded up, and what were once rooms filled with sunlight were now rooms filled with dust—lots and lots of dust. On June 24, the demolition work was complete; the entire house was gutted. Now we could build what we had dreamed of building for years.

Throughout the remodel, Steve hadn't been feeling well. Earlier in April, he had begun experiencing back and neck pain. We'd been traveling quite a bit, so we thought it was just the aches and pains from squeezing into small airplane seats. He began going to the chiropractor and felt some relief. The chiropractor had taken x-rays and said that his spine was in great condition; he just needed a few adjustments.

By May, the pain was increasing in his lower back, but the neck pain had gone away. Steve was uncomfortable but able to do his normal routine. He went to our GP, and she gave him some pain medication and ordered up blood and bone work. The results for both came back suggesting that he was in great health. Everything looked good. At that point, Steve felt he just needed to see a physical therapist to strengthen his back muscles and do what it took to get back into shape and feel good again.

By June, the increasing pain was beginning to interfere with Steve's daily activities. He was fatigued and didn't feel like himself. He was able to do what he wanted, and then without notice he would be sick and unable to get out of bed. The attacks would last a couple of hours, and then he would begin to recover.

On June 26, Steve and Sara were cleaning up left-behind boards and debris in our house. Together, the two of them lifted the heavy ones and took them to the dumpster in our driveway. As they tossed the final one, Steve collapsed in pain.

On June 30, the pain in his back was unbearable. A friend, Brad, was able to get us in to see a doctor at the Mayo Clinic. We felt like Steve had some sort of infection. We shared this with the doctor, and he thought that was a good possibility based on his symptoms. He examined him and said he looked great but suggested going upstairs to get an MRI. We were to come back at 4:00 for him to read the results.

At 4:00, we were back at his office, waiting for the MRI results and looking forward to figuring out what was going on. We so wanted to stop the pain and get back to life. The doctor walked in and said he had some very sad news. The MRI had revealed that Steve had cancerous tumors all up and down his spine. One of the tumors was so aggressive that it had fractured his L-4 vertebra, and that's where the pain was coming from. The MRI also revealed a mass, 5–6 centimeters in size, in the right lung, and that the lung was filled with fluid. It was clear that more tests were needed to determine where the cancer originated so that we could determine a treatment plan.

On July 1, we returned to the Mayo Clinic for more tests and made an appointment to meet with an oncology doctor after all the tests were completed. On July 9, we met with the oncologist. He told us that Steve's right lung was filled with cancer and that his left lung was perfectly healthy. Cancer had completely taken over the vertebrae in his back. He was diagnosed with Adenocarcinoma, a type of lung cancer. Steve was not a smoker.

At that point, the cancer hadn't spread to any other organs. The oncologist recommended that we see a radiologist immediately to help alleviate the pain. He said that the radiologist would probably recommend ten days of intense treatment and then begin chemotherapy. The goal of the chemotherapy would be to arrest and possibly shrink the tumor in his lung, in hopes of it not spreading to the rest of his body. That evening when we came home, Steve started taking morphine for his pain.

On July 13, we met with the radiologist and got a CAT Scan of Steve's brain. Great news—the cancer had not spread to his brain. When we received the news, Steve said, "This is cause for celebration! Morphine for everyone!" Steve started radiation a couple days later. It was our hope that the radiation would kill the tumors on his spine and alleviate the intense pain. Once the pain began to go away, in a couple of weeks, we would be able to cut back on the morphine. If all went well, Steve would move on to chemotherapy after the radiation treatments.

From July 16 to July 26, the radiation treatments went well. There were some good days and some bad days, but that was the nature of the disease. During the weeks of radiation, we hired people to help Steve continue the remodel, so the house was always busy with construction workers, and decisions had to be made constantly.

Steve ordered our hardwood floors from a barn in Pennsylvania; they were due to arrive in a couple of weeks. We also met with a guy to order the kitchen cabinets. Steve was a fabulous cook and was so excited to finally be able to design his dream kitchen. As we sat there making decisions, Steve stopped and ask me what color stain I wanted for the wood cabinets. This was his project. I knew he had it all figured out, but he looked at me with tender eyes and tried to engage me in the decisions. No way, this was his kitchen—he was going to get it just the way he wanted.

The beautiful wood ceilings were being installed, and the carpenter asked me what stain we wanted on the wood. Steve was resting in bed, so I went in and asked him what color he wanted. He said he wanted it to look just like sourdough toast, so I toasted some sourdough bread and handed it to the contractor.

CHAPTER ELEVEN
Time to Say Good-Bye

July 27, 2004. It was early in the morning, and the entire family was home. Amanda and Sara were back from college, and Makena was still sleeping. I woke up to Steve, lying in bed on his back, going through the motions of shooting a free throw. This was not normal, but nothing about our lives was normal anymore. For our family, normal was simply managing Steve's pain so that he could spend time with family and loved ones. He was heavily medicated with morphine and other drugs just to keep him comfortable.

Steve had been a member of three UCLA men's basketball NCAA Championship teams under Coach John Wooden, and the starting center on two of those squads. But what Steve gained from Coach Wooden had much more to do with living life than playing basketball.

It had been thirty-three years since he had practiced basketball with Coach Wooden at UCLA. Yet when his mind was trying to make sense of something that made no sense at all, Steve went back to practicing the fundamentals that he was taught as a young athlete. Year after year, Steve was blessed with people showing up in his life and coaching him on how to be his best. Some coaches spent years with him, some only moments, but their impact made him the man that he was—a man, very sick with cancer, still striving to be the best that he could be.

That morning when I saw Steve practicing free throws, I asked him what he was doing. He said that he was warming up for the game. I told him the game was over. He stopped, looked a bit confused, and then with a twinkle in his eyes, asked if we had won. With a smile of great love, I said, "Yes," and then he asked, with that same sparkle, "Did I make the first shot?"

I smiled and responded, "Yes, my dear, you did and you were great!"

A few moments passed, and I could tell he was processing his disconnected feelings. He evidently remembered the cardinal rule of always leaving the practice court after a made shot, because he emphatically asked, "Did I make the last shot?"

By this time, I was snuggled up to him, holding him and living in whatever moment he was in. I replied, "Yes, babe, you made the last shot, and we won the game."

The memory of that special moment never fades. I can feel his breath. I can see his smile. And that twinkle in his eyes is one of my favorite memories.

The day got progressively worse, and I called in our dear friends, Michelle and Larry, from Los Angeles to come help. They got on a plane and arrived in Phoenix within hours. When they arrived, Steve asked Larry to help him get his house in order. He took the tape measure and began telling Larry how he wanted everything completed. As I watched Steve fight to hold on to life, I went into our bedroom closet, shut the door, and cried. Steve heard me and opened the door. "Why are you crying?" he said. "Did someone hurt you? Please, babe, know I will always take care of you. Don't be afraid, and please don't cry. Let's go to the beach." Steve knew that was my favorite place, and to him it made perfect sense to head to the beach. I, on the other hand, not heavily medicated with morphine, did not want to go to the beach. Steve insisted, and what the heck, maybe an imaginary trip to the beach was just what we both needed. So we got in our car and pretended to drive to the beach. After a short drive, we returned home and Steve went to take a nap.

When he woke up, he said to me, "Get a paper and pen. I have something very important to tell you." He was standing in our bedroom, looking out our window. He said, "The chariot is coming for me. I must prepare." He then asked me help him pick out the right clothes. I reached for his jeans and T-shirt, and he told me that wasn't right, he needed to look his best. And then as he watched intensely out the window, he recited these words for me to write down:

"Foreshadowing the end of the war, we are declaring for we shall by reunite the United States of America on the North American continent. It has been a struggle, one under leadership and grace of a sovereign God and to him we pray our allegiance. It is not for us today to complete this action or the final details of this final victory. We are watched. I hereby proclaim and hereby pass the torch to the next generation to complete the task of unity, fidelity, humanity, and justice for all. In God's grace, amen. To this task we dedicate our lives and to the lives that have fallen to this idea. The idea is to declare it done."

Steve wanted to sign the document, and then he said he needed to rest and went back to bed.

When he woke up, he asked me where his basketball uniform was because he had a game today. I reminded him that the game was over and that we had won. He was wearing just his boxers and proceeded to leave the bedroom. Sara and her friend, Samantha, were in the front room, and they asked where he was going as he headed out the front door, me following behind, trying to get him to stop. He told them he had a game. I told him again that we had won the game. Not believing me, he asked Sara if we had won the game. She said yes. He then asked what the score was. She made up some number, and he was satisfied. As he turned to come back in the house, he told all of us to gather around because we needed to pray. Keep in mind we had concrete and dirt floors, and he had a broken back. He instructed us all to circle up, and we knelt down, holding hands. Steve always prayed for our family, yet this time, he started to pray and then stopped and said to me, "Mama, you pray for us." And so we all prayed, and then he went back to bed.

Steve and I had never talked about him dying. I never wanted to think it was even a possibility. I knew that God would heal him; I clung to that belief with every fiber of my body. Friends and family were gathering and doing their best to prepare me for Steve's final days. I couldn't believe it was happening. How could a strong, healthy man go from coaching a boys' basketball team one month to dying of cancer the next? It was too much to comprehend, and my heart didn't want to let him go. But Steve was letting go. He was saying his goodbyes, and I knew he needed me to let him go.

As I sat in bed with Steve, I told him it would be okay for him to go, that we would be okay. I said all the things the hospice nurse told me to say so that Steve would be released to do what he needed to do. I was strong, and I didn't want him to be in pain. The last month had been a nightmare, consumed with trips to the hospital, huge doses of medication, and him crying out in pain. I wanted the nightmare to end. I did love him enough to let him go. At least that's what my mind kept telling me, and for his sake, I so wanted to believe it. I could do anything for him, including letting him die if that was God's will.

He woke up from his rest and asked to see Makena. She bounced in, so happy to see her daddy. We lifted her up and cradled her in his arms. Together they sang their song. "Yes, sir, she's my babe. No, sir, I don't mean maybe. Yes, sir, she's my baby girl." He kissed her, and she hopped down, ready to go back out and play. That was the last time her daddy held her.

The day turned to night, and we all gathered around to enjoy a wonderful bottle of wine that Larry and Michelle had brought. Steve drank a couple of glasses and enjoyed every sip with his friends and family. That was our last night together.

The night was long and painful. We all knew the end was close. Steve lay in bed, and his brother, Bob, and I sat in chairs beside him. We kept the door to our bedroom closed. Steve's mom and Amanda came in to say good-bye. Sara wasn't ready to let him go; she was very angry at me because I had told her he wouldn't die. The night turned into day, and everything moved in slow motion.

It was awful watching Steve die. Death is so ugly and cruel. And then in the middle of the morning, on July 28th, he reached his arms up and started moving his legs like he was climbing. I screamed, not knowing what he was doing. I was afraid he was going to fall out of bed. And then it got quiet. He took a few more breaths and then no more. In those moments when the dreadful sound of him struggling to breathe stopped, a peace filled the room. It was beyond anything I have words to describe, but it was beautiful. I could feel Jesus in our bedroom, coming to take Steve home. *Really, God, you love us this much that you would come to our bedroom and take your son, Steve Patterson, home to be with you?* I was in awe of God's love for us in that moment.

I walked out of the bedroom, closing the door behind me. There was Sara, ready to say her good-byes, but it was too late — he was already gone.

Everyone left so that the girls and I could be alone for a while. Amanda, Sara, and I snuggled up in bed with Steve and held him. It was wonderful. It was peaceful and so very special. From the moment he took his last breath, he looked beautiful. In that moment, the cancer left his body and he looked like himself again. He was healed. He was with Jesus, and we knew it.

CHAPTER TWELVE
July 28, 2004
Dear Steve

Steve didn't necessarily know the depth of the words he found the courage to write to me or how they would be played out in our future. All he knew was that he needed me to know how he felt...

> *I <u>know</u> my work here and now is nearly done. What lies ahead? I have given it little thought. Have had little time to give it thought. I have little cared to give it thought, and here <u>you</u> come. Or maybe it's just really me. Its readiness, it's longing. That is what I wonder.*
>
> *I have long believed, but little spoke of true love and passion and meaning in relationship. I gave it up with the bloom of youth for the hard reality of obligation and commitment. I have no regrets. I am proud of my work, my life, my family. I have achieved much in an area where many fail, or fail to try. I have the peace that comes from having given your best whatever the outcome. (Sounds like John Wooden!)*
>
> *<u>Nothing</u> can separate you from my love for you. Not time, or distance, or work or deed. I am devoted to your happiness and prosperity and the future of your little ones. Please make any request that you wish and test my devotion to you.*
>
> *I embrace you.*
>
> *S*

The tenderness of those words came from Steve's heart and soul, and nothing, not even death, could end our love. On July 28, 2004, as I sat alone in a quiet room visited by death, I reached for pen and paper to share my heart with Steve.

To My Husband...

When the invariable waves of life came crashing in, Steve never felt they were too big to handle. And the small pebbles that the waves swept to shore were never too small. Great food. Great wine. Great family. Great joy. He embraced the romance of life and the rigors of life. It was wine on the beach and battle in the foxholes. He was fierce in competition, but gentle in nature. Steve was the Keeper of our Castle: the Warrior and the Winner.

Steve was a man of gentle greatness. Greatness is built upon the staples — an unrelenting mastery of the basics and faithfulness in the small things. Steve was never too busy to read Makena a story every night, to faithfully prepare gourmet meals for his family, or to unselfishly volunteer to coach the girls' sports teams in practice after practice.

Greatness is built upon Standards — holding to a strong code of ethics and living them.

Steve's standards were high and his expectations of their attainment were just as high. Like the strong oarsman, he spent his life pursuing mastery and skill. Even if he wasn't good at something, he would work at it until he was. If there was a task he didn't know how to do, he simply said, "If that is what is expected of me, I will become great at it." He shrank from nothing, was deterred by nothing, and quit at nothing.

Steve stood tall and he also stood firm. His standards were high and his values were deep. He was a solid man—feet squarely planted on the firm foundation—solid stone—bedrock values—of charitableness, chivalry, and consistency.

And finally, greatness is built upon Stature — the watermark that sets the indelible "reach point." Stature is measured by strength of character and strength of purpose. The stature of a man is not what he has, but what he has given. Steve lived to recognize the tireless harvest worker, to inspire the discouraged athlete, to embrace the meaningful cause. He was a man of his word, a man of wisdom, and a man of watchfulness.

Like the revolving lighthouse beam, he habitually scanned life's terrain, looking for opportunities to illuminate others' contributions. Steve often felt credited for harvests that, in actuality, included the efforts of many, many other people. John 4:35 was one of his favorite scriptures: "Behold I say to you, lift up your eyes and look at the fields, for they are already white for harvest! And he who reaps receives wages, and gathers fruit for eternal life, that both he who sows and he who reaps may rejoice together. For in this the saying is true: 'One sows and another reaps.' I sent you to reap that for which you have not labored; others have labored, and you have entered into their labors."

Steve splashed selflessness, kindness and an inherent goodness on every encounter he had with others. He sought to encourage, inspire, and give. Steve left large footprints in the sands of our lives. Steve's stature is measured by his investment in and influence on other people. By conscious design, Steve chose a life whose flow was not inward-bound, but influence-bound — a presence that rippled into many lives for many years.

Steve was a man of gentle greatness. Steve lived excellence. May the Lord say to my husband, to Dad, to our friend, to Coach Patterson, "Well Done, Good and Faithful Servant."

With all my love,

C

CHAPTER THIRTEEN
Now What?

Steve had died. No more making sure he had his medicine at the right time, no more hoping he would have a good moment so we could share a conversation, no more holding hands to give each other strength. It all happened so fast.

It was time for the funeral home to come and take Steve's body from our bedroom. Nothing can prepare you for those men showing up with a stretcher and a body bag. I didn't want Amanda and Sara to see, but I couldn't get them to leave Steve's side. I had to carry Sara out of our bedroom. She was screaming and hysterical. "No, Mom! Don't let them take him!" I'll never forget those words. I got her to her room, and I lay with her for a few minutes as the men waited inside our bedroom for me to okay them taking Steve away. I wanted to stay in her bedroom forever if that would keep them from taking Steve, but it was time.

My parents took Makena back to their hotel; she too was crying and screaming at me. Her face was pierced up against the car window glass, and she was screaming, "Mommy, I don't want to go! Mommy, help me!" Another picture in my mind that never fades. She had no idea why she was so sad or why she didn't want to go, but in her heart, she knew something was terribly wrong. She didn't know that her Daddy had died. She wouldn't even have known what those words meant. I needed time to figure out how to tell her, what to tell her — and right then wasn't the time.

Amanda was curled up in the fetal position in my office with Michelle, my friend that God tapped on the shoulder and asked to stand beside me as I entered into the darkest days of my life. Amanda was scared. She didn't know what to do or how to act; it was all too much for her to grasp. The house was filled with family and with strangers, and the four people that Amanda relied on to make sure she was okay were not okay anymore. I couldn't even get to Amanda; I trusted Michelle to take care of her.

I walked down the hall to our bedroom to see my husband's body being zipped up in a body bag. Life as we knew it was gone. They took him down the hall, out the front door, and loaded him into a car. I walked with him. I wanted to make sure they were gentle. I wanted to make sure he was okay. Crazy, I know, but just hours earlier, he had been there on earth. As they were struggling to get him into the car, a curl of his hair made its way out of the zipped up bag — such a harsh reminder that Steve, my husband, my little women's Daddy, was in that bag.

They drove away. I now had to go back into our home and deal with all the What Next. Michelle took over, and every detail went through her. She was such a gift from God. She comforted my little woman when I had to go make funeral arrangements. She sat with me and led me through all the decisions I had to make. I knew I could trust her to make sure I was making the right choices. As emotional of a time as this was, I had to make huge decisions quickly. Construction workers were still working in the house. If we stopped the construction, they would have to move on to another project and who knew when we would get back on their schedule. I decided to have them keep working.

My time with Michelle went something like this: what casket do you want to buy for Steve, what church do you want me to book for the service, how many hours do you want for the viewing, what finish do you want on your dishwasher, what oven do you want me to order, what size microwave do you want. . .the list was endless. It was dreadful.

CHAPTER FOURTEEN
Monterey

Where did I want to bury Steve? We had never talked about that, and I had no idea what to do. Michelle drove me around to all the cemeteries in Phoenix. We would get out, have a dreadful meeting with their staff, get back in the car, and I would say, "No way."

On the way home from the last cemetery visit, Michelle said, "You have to make a decision and choose one."

I said, "No way. These are all awful."

We drove some more, and then she gently asked me, over and over, where the perfect place for him was. She understood that I didn't want to make the decision because it meant admitting that Steve was really dead. After more gentle encouragement from her, I finally said, "Post Ranch Inn." It was my favorite place, a romantic, secluded resort in Big Sur, California. "What do you mean, Post Ranch Inn?" she said. "I want to bury him in the closest cemetery to Post Ranch Inn." So she called Post Ranch Inn and asked where the closest cemetery was. They had no idea; they had never been asked that question before.

We got home, and Michelle went on the Internet and found the closest cemetery to Post Ranch Inn. She called them and found a plot for Steve. We chose one under a tree. I wanted him to be buried there because I knew that the only way Makena was going to know her daddy would be from us going to visit his grave. I wanted his grave to be someplace that we loved.

Days later, after the Celebration of Life ceremony we held for Steve in Phoenix, our family boarded a plane for Monterey. We landed and found our way to the hotel. The girls stayed with my family, and I went to visit the cemetery for the first time. As I drove into the very unfamiliar place, I felt waves of sadness wash over me. For the first time since Steve died, I was alone. I wasn't taking care of my family or answering questions or praying to God to help me not lose it. I had taken care of everything. It was the last event for Steve.

As I drove through the small streets of the cemetery lined with headstones, I found my way to the big tree that marked the plot we had chosen for Steve. I pulled up to the fresh grave that had a small, simple sign that said Steve Patterson. Someone from the cemetery brought me a simple, white folding chair, and I sat there. I could hear the sounds of children playing in the playground across the street. Months earlier, as a family, we had stopped at that playground to swing, to laugh, to hang out. The air was cool, fresh, and familiar — such a welcome change from the scorching heat of Phoenix in July.

I knew this place, it was our place. We loved going to Monterey and Carmel; it was so familiar. My heart, my mind, my soul, each one tried to make sense of the sounds, the memories, the disorientation that I felt. The family would be waiting for me to go to dinner, so I needed to tuck my heart back into a safe, guarded place and go through the motions of another surreal task on this journey of saying good-bye.

After dinner, the girls and I went back to our hotel room. I wanted to hold them and tell them it was going to be okay, but I couldn't — because I didn't know if it was going to be okay. I wanted to cry, I wanted to run away, I wanted to rewind time and make it not happen, but I couldn't. It was real. The pain in my little women's eyes was so piercing, at times I felt like my heart was going to stop beating. The pain penetrated every coping mechanism I drew on to survive, and nothing was working anymore. I quietly slipped into the bathroom and ran the bath water. Once the sound of the water was going, I quietly wept.

The morning came, and I got up early so I could go be with Steve at his grave. There were chairs set up in front of his casket. I sat there looking at the casket, trying to remember to breathe. It was quiet and peaceful. I could feel God's presence, and I knew we had picked the perfect place for Steve and for me, when my time comes. I wanted to sit there forever so that they wouldn't bury Steve. I didn't want to say good-bye. I didn't want to leave him there buried in the ground and go back to Phoenix to live a life that we created but without "we" anymore. And then a gentle touch of a stranger's hand brought me back to the gravesite. He had a few questions for me before the ceremony began.

I went back to the hotel to be with my little women and my family. We prepared for the reception and went through the mundane motions of preparing for the burial. I don't remember what time it was or how we got to the cemetery, but I do remember sitting there and feeling peaceful. No one knew why I had picked that cemetery, but as we all sat there — the ocean waves crashing in the background, the beautiful redwood trees towering over us — everyone said it was the perfect place for Steve. In my heart and soul, I agreed.

We said good-bye to my husband, to a father, to a son, to a brother, to a friend, to a man that wanted more life and was blessed with eternity too soon.

CHAPTER FIFTEEN
A Very Thin Veil

The girls and I returned home from Monterey to an empty, gutted house — boarded up windows, a dirt floor, and flowers and plants everywhere from the funeral. It was a dreadful homecoming. It was sad, overwhelming, and hopeless. I had no idea how I was going to put the house back together, raise our five-year-old daughter alone, and deal with Amanda and Sara's anger and pain because another Daddy had left them. All I wanted to do was pack my bags and move to Monterey. How in the world did God expect me to do it?

The days slowly passed. Amanda and Sara went back to college. Makena and I got to work figuring out how to put the house back together. Every day, the contractors arrived at 7:00 a.m. and then spent the day hammering and tearing up things, leaving dust and dirt everywhere. I had to make decisions about where to put walls, what sink and countertops we wanted, what to do with the list of things that were not going right—huge decisions, big financial decisions — but if I stopped, the contractors would stop and our home would not get put back together.

The wood floors arrived, and the truck driver asked for Steve Patterson to sign for them. It was hard to believe that he had ordered them and then died. But they arrived, the floor that he wanted for our home. As I signed for them, I could hear us talking about them, looking at them on the Web and enjoying the story of where the wood came from and why Steve wanted us to have that particular wood in our home. Steve was meticulous about every detail. At times it was overwhelming to me, but never to him. He found such satisfaction in knowing that he had checked out every option, thought about each one, and then made the best decision. I had learned to find comfort in knowing that everything we did had a lengthy story behind it and that Steve had paid attention to every aspect of the story before he had made a commitment for us to add that story to ours.

Life with a home full of contractors became the norm. Their noise filled my silent, empty world. Their constant questions kept me connected to Steve as I thought back to what he had said he was going to do about that particular issue, and then I was able to direct them accordingly. Day by day, the house was changing, and I was too. There were some decisions Steve and

I hadn't talked about — we hadn't gotten to those yet — so I had to think about what I wanted, just me, not what Steve and I wanted. Those simple decisions began slowly directing me to find me, not we.

Lost in the void of survival, I was not much of a mom for Amanda and Sara. I was doing all that I could to hold myself together and really wasn't doing too good of a job at all. I was struggling to make sense of why a God that loves us so much would do what he did to our family. My brain, my body, and my heart ached in a way I hadn't thought was possible. It was too much. I couldn't do it, yet I couldn't figure out how not to do it either.

I missed Steve so much, but I could feel him with me. I could feel his presence. I started to find comfort in connecting with him in a very different way. I felted incredibly loved by him. I felt the purity of our love story all over again, without the interference of the world. Our relationship was peaceful again. We were connected, yet he was gone. I wondered if that was what having a relationship with God was like. I had never seen God, yet I could feel his love for me. I found comfort in God, and now I was finding moments of comfort when I would disappear into my thoughts and find Steve.

I wondered if that was why it's been said that the veil between life on earth and in heaven is paper thin. I was beginning to get a true sense of it. In one minute, Steve was gasping for every breath — and then in a moment, it was quiet. He didn't need air anymore. He was gone. Our life together on earth was over, just like that. One minute he was here, and the next minute he was gone. Yet his body was still there, and our life was still there. But nothing would ever be the same. It was as if a whisper of air had blown the veil, and Steve's time on earth was over. Yet I still could feel Steve, and I felt like we communicated. He answered every question I asked him. He was always there for me; all I had to do was call his name. It was just like Steve to bless me with a glimpse of heaven so I would know that everything we prayed for and believed in was real and true. I knew that Steve was with Jesus. I knew it like I knew I had three daughters. It was as real to me as life itself, and for that I give huge thanks and praise to our almighty God.

The connection I had with Steve brought me great comfort and provided me with hope that I too would spend eternity with Jesus, and that our girls would join us as well. But it didn't take away the excruciating pain of the loss of life together. It was the reality of our separation that was so painful. My heart knew where to find comfort, but my mind knew my work on earth was not over. I had three little women to raise, and I was committed to doing that until God calls me home. I guarded my heart and prayed for it to keep beating so that I could be there for my little women.

FIVE IN A ROW FOR UCLA

Sports Illustrated
APRIL 5, 1971   60 CENTS

**STEVE PATTERSON
UNEXPECTED HERO**

CHAPTER SIXTEEN
Steve's Story

Looking back, I'm not able to explain exactly how this happened, but in Steve's last days, he was able to tell his story. Steve and I were involved in Sports Ministries. One of them was called TheGoal.com, and its mission is to have professional athletes share their life stories. Somewhere in the chaos of Steve's last twenty-eight days on earth, Dave Hood, founder of TheGoal.com, called and asked if he could come and talk to Steve about his story.

I don't remember how many days Dave spent at our home waiting patiently for Steve to have a clear moment so they could talk. We never knew what the day would bring. Without explanation, "normal" moments would appear, and then quietly the two of them, Dave with pen, paper, recorder, and camera, would disappear into the memories that Steve wanted to share. What a gift from God for us to have Steve's story as he wanted to tell it before his last chapter was written, only days later.

> *Steve was an extraordinary man. An athlete and an historian, a father and a husband, a visionary and a Christian, Steve touched the lives of many people.*
>
> *During the days leading up to his death, on July 28, 2004, Steve shared his thoughts about sports and life and dying and faith and family... The following is a paraphrased transcript of his thoughts.*
> *Written by Dave Hood, of TheGoal.com*

Steve Patterson
I am the answer to an intriguing trivia question.

"Who was the starting center at UCLA between Lew Alcindor, who became Kareem Abdul-Jabbar, and Bill Walton?"

That would be me—Steve Patterson.

While I certainly wasn't the player Lew and Bill were—in fact, my sophomore year I was a "human victory cigar," meaning Coach Wooden would only put me in when the game was not in jeopardy — nonetheless, my years at UCLA were so formative for everything I was to become.

I was in the premier college basketball program in the country, playing against the best players in the world — not during games, but during practices. I played against Lew Alcindor more than anyone on earth. I was 6'9", and he was 7'2". It was a struggle. At first I was confident, but after a while I became a bit demoralized. I found myself thinking, "Lew is either the best player who's ever lived, or I'm lousy."

It was always at the times I was most discouraged that John Wooden would say to me, "Just be ready. Your time will come."

It did.

I was the starting center my junior and senior years at UCLA, when we won two more national championships. My last game at UCLA was against Villanova, in 1971, for the national championship. While I had games I thought were better, many pointed to that particular game as my best at UCLA — 29 points and 8 rebounds.

The next year, I was the first pick in the second round, going to the Cleveland Cavaliers. I played with the Cavaliers for four full years, and in the fifth year, I was traded to the Chicago Bulls for Nate Thurmond.

I was a journeyman player, but the exciting thing about being in the NBA was simply being on the floor, competing with the best players in the world — people like Jerry West, Willis Reed, John Havlicek, and Dave Cowens. It was a humbling experience to jump center against the likes of Wilt Chamberlain. Physically, I wasn't big enough; strong enough; quick enough; or athletic enough; but I worked hard and was always prepared, like Coach Wooden had taught me, and had a wonderful experience.

While I had many other wonderful experiences, serving as CEO of Super Bowl XXX, Commissioner of the CBA, Executive Director of the Grand Canyon State Games, my highest calling in life has been to be a follower of Jesus Christ.

I was very fortunate to grow up in a strong, Christian home. At a very early age, maybe 10 or 11, I recognized the offering of eternal life and accepted Jesus as my Savior.

Church was a big part of my life through high school and college. But my experience was similar to many growing up in a Christian home. I trusted God for my eternal salvation but did not trust Him with the details of my daily life.

Since I had very little adversity in my life, the reality of a daily walk with God did not seem to be a requirement. Then, at UCLA, things got a bit tougher. I took an anthropology course and began to go through a process of checking in with my faith. The question became whether my faith would hold up in the real world. UCLA became a crucible for my faith. I really relied on the Lord to sustain me, despite what those around me were saying.

Then, when I went to Cleveland and the NBA, I became a bit complacent. My ego got the better of me. The adulation and glory were intoxicating. I believed it was all about me, and not about the Lord, and began to rely on my own strength.

When I did experience some real adversity, I found myself turning to the Lord again. In fact, that became the pattern. I'd become complacent, experience adversity, draw close again, until the adversity had passed, and then I'd become complacent again. I needed to learn to be obedient regardless of the circumstances.

My turning point came after my playing days. I totally surrendered. I became honest with myself and honest with God and acknowledged that if it was up to me to keep the faith; I wouldn't be able to do it. That was my watershed.

Since that time there have been ups and downs in terms of work and family and life, but the one thing that has sustained me through it all has been my faith.

I never understood the grace of Jesus Christ until I stopped fighting it and simply accepted it. That's when I found a total peace.

While I might be the answer to a trivia question, there is nothing trivial about grace. In fact, it's the most profound thing I've ever experienced.

Early Influence

Steve pointed to three men as having great influence in his life. One was his father. The other two were coaches — Bob McCutcheon and John Wooden.

Steve said, "I'm a firm believer that the mark of the man is not that he is the biggest or the fastest or the strongest. My father was kind and gentle and self-effacing. He put others first and taught me not to go solo. That's the real mark of a man." It was through his father that Steve learned of salvation through the grace of God.

While many fathers read to their children, their reading material is usually limited to children's stories. Not so in the Patterson household. Steve remembers his father reading to him from a classic book, "As a Man Thinketh." The 'little volume,' as the author, James Allen, calls it, formed the basis for much of Steve's thinking and the tone of the book could be heard as an echo in Steve's thoughtful and articulated conversation as an adult.

Bob McCutcheon, Steve's high school coach, was the first to point out to Steve all the potential and the vast horizon that lay before him. "Coach said, 'I see great things for you.' My father was a humble man who expected excellence but didn't demand greatness. Coach McCutcheon was the first one to tell me I could achieve something great.

"It was completely liberating, and impossible to describe the power his encouragement gave me."

And then there was Coach Wooden — the legend — the Wizard of Westwood. Steve knew he was blessed to have been a student of Coach Wooden's.

Reflecting on his days at UCLA, where he was surrounded by and practiced against teammates who would go on to be some of the greatest players in the NBA, Steve sometimes felt out-classed. "It was a situation where it makes you better or kills you. More than once I thought it would kill me. Others would mock me and laugh at me, and there were times when I was awkward and less than glamorous. But Coach lifted me up.

"I could probably write a book on going through difficulty, and some of that difficulty was at UCLA. I had to be content with little victories. The team had already won national championships. The players were the best.

Being Ready

"At the right moment, Coach Wooden would say to me, 'If you are ready, your time will come.'"

"It went from possibility to probability to reality."

"Playing at UCLA and being part of the string of championships, even though I was the center on the team Coach Wooden referred to as the team with no center, was so precious. I felt I had earned something very rare. It wasn't given to me — I worked for it."

"And having Coach encourage me to be ready for my time to come is something that has grown in value for me over the years."

In his typical way, Steve made a connection between what he learned as an athlete, and his faith. Thinking how Coach Wooden had quietly encouraged him to be ready for his time, Steve said, "Maybe we don't do enough of that. Maybe Christians don't whisper in ears enough, offering encouragement and assurance that, in time, things will work out. We want it all now. Sometimes we have to wait, and while we wait, we get ready."

The Bridge

Steve was a bridge. He was a bridge between two of the greatest college centers to ever play the game — Lew Alcindor (Kareem Abdul-Jabbar) and Bill Walton.

He was also a bridge in a more metaphorical way. He saw himself as a connecting point between sports and faith. He was an athlete, and competed on the highest level and the largest stage, but he was first and foremost a Christian.

At times being both an athlete and a Christian was difficult for Steve. He struggled with what he called the dichotomy between faith in Jesus and athletic competition. As a thoughtful person, he occasionally struggled as he attempted to reconcile his place in athletics with his faith. "It tore me apart," he said, speaking of his own internal struggle to blend competition with faith, "It probably kept me from developing the kind of profound relationship I both wanted and needed with God."

Yet Steve recognized the important place sports has always had in the world-wide culture, even from the Greek and Roman periods. Being both a Christian and an athlete carried with it, for Steve, a set of ethics above and beyond those standards and ethics that most follow.

Calling

Reconciling sports and faith became Steve's life passion. Being in sports ministry was something Steve found liberating, and provided a sense of integration in his own life. "God is calling me," Steve said with utter certainty, "to bring my sports experience and contacts and my competitive instincts to serve the Kingdom of God."

Steve had felt God's hand upon his life at an early age. "I went to church and Sunday School, in fact my high school coach was my Sunday School teacher. I learned to be in the world without being of the world. I was taught a Kingdom perspective. I always felt I had been set apart — set apart by

God, which caused some resentment on the part of my peers.

"But I always felt God had a purpose for my life — maybe a moment, or a series of moments — in which I could proclaim the Gospel on His behalf.

"I take responsibility for proclaiming the Gospel very seriously, because it's such an awesome task. It's an awesome task to always be prepared to give an accounting of yourself—why your yea is yea and your nay is nay.

"Now that I am retired from basketball I've been able to work out a more consistent platform to share my faith, within a context in which God would have me share it.

"The opportunities to proclaim the Gospel go on and on, if we are faithful."

Professionalism

Speaking about what it means to be a "professional" basketball player, Steve went beyond the superficial element of pay. "A professional," he said, "has a craft and has mastered that craft to such a degree that it separates him with respect to others. The professional has the attributes and the qualifications and the training to overcome challengers unique to extraordinary events and extraordinary times."

"Being a professional is more than having talent. Talent alone does not always suffice. Talent can be insufficient due to a lack of training."

Again, Steve made the connection between the sports world and faith. He compared the attributes of a "professional" athlete with those of a mature disciple.

"The correlation is to the disciple, who has talents and has trained those talents through exposure to grace and to the Word of God, and who has the calling — who has felt the calling and heard the calling to be a servant of God — and is prepared for the unique demands of extraordinary times."

"Perhaps we've developed an understanding of Christianity that is too trite. A "pro" is set apart — so is a disciple of Jesus."

Sacrifice

Again drawing parallels between sports and faith, Steve spoke of teamwork. In fact, one of Steve's often-repeated expressions was, "God is a Team — Don't Go Solo."

According to Steve, there is no success without teamwork. It's possible to have all the individual accolades and still not win. Teamwork requires a mental mindset of sacrifice — being able to give up what's in your own individual interest for the sake of the team.

In fact, in Steve's viewpoint, there is no success without individual sacrifice — not only in team sports, but in life. "To win you must lose," he said, and talked about the concept of harvest, of dying and rebirth.

In some ways playing at UCLA, in such a team-minded system, created a dilemma. The team took precedence over the individual, and yet the pro teams were looking for individual games. "There were games when I didn't have the statistics, but did what I needed to do to help us win. That's what winning as a team meant."

This concept of sacrifice for the greater good of the team is something he especially learned from Coach Wooden. But Steve took it to another level, and made the connection with faith. "Ultimately," he said, "It boils down to whether a man will give his life, as a mustard seed placed into the ground. When that happens, God gives him his life back again, with even greater force, and he lives powerfully, both now and for eternity."

While Steve came to faith at an early age, his faith was honed and sharpened during his time at UCLA, both by learning from Coach Wooden and by being involved in faith enterprises.

Steve talked about two such faith enterprises during his college years that had great bearing on the man he would become.

One was at Hume Lake, a Christian conference grounds. He worked as a night watchman, and would spend evening after evening contemplating issues large and small. "I realized," he said, "that in regard to life I needed to take a larger view. It wasn't just about me, and it wasn't about basketball. It was about Jesus."

The other experience through which Steve was shaped while at UCLA was his involvement in JC Light and Powerhouse, which he referred to as a "counter-cultural takeoff on the early church." The concept of this somewhat radical campus ministry was to blend faith into modern living — an idea which stayed with Steve the rest of his life.

While Steve's accomplishments were many — ranging from being Commissioner of the CBA and CEO of Super Bowl XXX and Executive Director of the Grand Canyon State Games, he was first and foremost a disciple of Jesus Christ — a fact which shaped and formed his relationships with his family and friends, associates and co-workers.

His life was rich and full — "robust" was the word he often used — and it was all based on his understanding of grace — the unconditional love of God upon which he learned to rely.

He was faithful to the end.

When the Time Comes

Steve's thoughts on the focus required to be a "professional" seem an apt way to remember him.

For Steve, the key to being a "professional," whether as an athlete or a disciple, was focus. Making a free throw is easy. Making a free throw in a pressure packed situation is not. A skill or an attribute, whether in sports or faith, can be lost because of a lack of focus. Steve found that focus came through practice. "Coach Wooden was a firm believer in practice. He used to tell me, 'If you practice, your time will come. If you don't practice, your time will come and you won't be ready.'"

"I've seen that principle demonstrated time and again in my life, in sports as well as in my faith. Focus refines a skill, and focus comes through practice. I saw it at Super Bowl XXX. There were all these things that had to happen at a certain time, and they had been rehearsed and rehearsed, and we were ready.

"Focus is about being ready in the moment. St. Paul said it well, 'Putting aside every weight I press on toward the goal.' That's focus. Putting every obstacle and every distraction aside, and being in the moment.

"The outcome will be achieved if you are ready in each moment."

On July 28, 2004, God called Steve Patterson's name, and Steve was ready.

CHAPTER SEVENTEEN
UCLA Reunion

It had been one month to the day that Steve died. We were scheduled to go to a UCLA reunion on September 28th. The UCLA family expressed their deep sorrow and their love for Steve and our family. If at all possible, they still wanted me to come if I could. Steve's death had happened so quickly it was hard for everyone to believe. As a way for all of us to make sense of it, we cherished time together to share Steve memories. It felt right to be with the UCLA family as we all stumbled through the shock of Steve being gone. So Sara and I went to the reunion. It was nice to be around all of Steve's teammates. It was so comforting to hear stories about him, to hear people say his name. It felt like he was not forgotten. I so did not want him to be forgotten, and he was beginning to feel further away from me.

During the reunion, they asked if I would share Steve's last twenty-eight days. They too wanted the sad story to make some sense. Perhaps hearing it from me, they could find peace with it. As I stood in front of the microphone and looked out at all the faces of people that Steve had grown up with, I wondered if they knew how powerful their time together in the UCLA gym had been in shaping Steve's life. He had discovered so much about himself with those guys, his teammates and coaches. Could they have ever imagined this day, thirty-three years later, with one teammate gone? Could they have known that playing a small role in something so much bigger than themselves took on meaning far greater than their championship basketball games?

Without effort, I began to share Steve's last chapter. The simple memories of how one minute Steve was coaching a boys' basketball team, his back started to hurt, and then...

I shared the intimate moments of Steve lying in bed shooting free throws and talking about winning the game. I wanted Steve's teammates to know that Steve went back to the days that he was with them, playing ball with Coach Wooden, during his final days on earth. The time that they spent in a college gym was part of his DNA; it made him the man that he was, and I loved that man.

I also shared how beautiful it was when Jesus came into our bedroom and escorted Steve home. I wanted them to have hope for their lives and to know that how they spent their time was important. *Don't waste another moment on things that don't matter. Get to know God. He loves you. He will be there for you too, when your time on earth is over.*

After I spoke, Coach Wooden gave me a hug and sat down with me. I asked him how he handled life without his wife; she too had died of cancer. He said something to me that I have never forgotten. He said you don't ever get over them, you just get through the very difficult time of grief. I asked him how, and he shared with me that on every anniversary of the day that Nell died, he wrote her a love letter. I hugged him and told him that I was going to figure out a way to get through this too. I thanked him for how much he loved Steve and for playing such a huge role in making him the man that I got to love.

CHAPTER EIGHTEEN
Six O'clock

Steve and Makena had a very special, close relationship. They "got" each other. Every night at 6:00, they would begin their nightly ritual of preparing dinner. Steve would transition from his work day to family time by opening a bottle of wine, sitting Makena up on the counter, and the two of them figuring out what cooking delight they were going to create. Makena had a little apron and chef's hat that she wore proudly as she sat on the counter, sipping juice from her Sippy cup, toasting to Dad with his wine glass.

Once Steve and Makena went into the kitchen for the evening, whatever had happened during the day disappeared, and our home filled with love. The house would be filled with the warm smells of garlic and olive oil simmering. Steve was always trying something new, looking for that perfect blend of flavors that would make all of his little women happy.

And then, July 28th, 2004 happened. Makena had just turned five in June. She was so mad at me for Steve dying. She didn't know what happened to her daddy, but she wanted him back. Her young brain couldn't comprehend how suddenly her daddy stopped showing up — to cook dinner, to read stories, to play. Nothing. He was gone. We told her about how he was in heaven with Jesus and read her books about where he had gone, but nothing worked.

It took a week or two before I noticed the very predictable nightmare that occurred every night at 6:00. Makena didn't know how to tell time, but every night, without fail, at 6:00 she would scream and cry and hit me, yelling at me to bring back her daddy. She would say how she wished I died, not him. Her words were so cruel, but it wasn't her words that hurt. She was just expressing herself like the rest of us wished we could. It hurt because I didn't have any answers for her. I couldn't help her in any way. No matter what I did, I couldn't comfort her. It was torture for Amanda, Sara, and me to go through that every single night like clockwork.

I talked to grief counselors, and they assured me that this behavior was normal and that as long as I let her work through it, it would pass. Oh my goodness, I so hoped that I could make it through her working her way through it. We were all a mess, and by the end of each day, none of us had anything left to give. It took every bit of energy just to do the basic things needed to function. I wouldn't say we got used to Makena terrorizing us every night, but it did become part of our nightly routine. The rage, the sadness, the words, they didn't change. I just sat with her and held her. Sometimes I cried, but most of all I prayed for God to please help our family.

We did art therapy, we did grief counseling, we did anything I could find to — please, dear God — bring us some relief from the awful pain of missing Steve. Amanda, Sara, and I did not like our counseling — it was so sad to talk about Steve dying — but Makena loved going to counseling. So we all would go, as a family, in hopes that the 6:00 terror would stop. But it didn't. I learned through our counseling how important it is for children to be able to go to group therapy when someone close to them dies. Being around other kids who've had a loved one die helps makes them feel normal again. This is because when their life suddenly changed, none of their friends' lives changed. They still had their daddy, and so instead of feeling good when Makena went over to play with her friends, she got sad and mad because she didn't have her daddy anymore. Wow, so many layers of pain and confusion happen when death rocks your world. Week after week, we were learning about how to cope in our new life. It was not pretty, it was sad, it was uncomfortable, but it was our new life and I had to figure out how to help my little women navigate through their grief.

After months of 6:00 terror, one night we were bringing in groceries — it was 6:00 — and it was quiet. Amanda, Sara, and I looked at each other. Then we looked at the clock and held our breath. We had gotten used to our nightly thirty minutes of torture, Makena expressing her feelings, telling me how much she hated me. Tonight was different. Oh, dear God, is this part of the grieving over, please? It was. It never happened again.

Our days were still filled with sadness, but sometimes we found something that brought a few minutes of distraction. The grief stuff was tough, and worst of all, we never knew when it was going to show up. Once I was in a grocery store and I saw a daddy with his daughter buying groceries. They reminded me so much of the way Steve and Makena looked together. I felt so sick, I thought I was going to pass out. I ran out of the store and dreaded ever going back. That happened all the time. Steve and I had lived in Phoenix for over twenty years, so there were a lot of places that held a lot of memories. I had to find a way to make friends with grief. I knew it was going to be a part of our lives forever.

Some days were tougher than others. Sometimes out of the blue we would just become too sad to keep going. So I started calling those days and moments Tender Heart Days/Moments. That gave us a language that fit how our hearts were feeling without having to go into detail about why we were struggling. It didn't matter why; all that mattered was that we got through it. The best cure for a Tender Heart Day or Moment was a hug, a simple acknowledgment that we missed Steve, but we were still loved and together we would figure out how to do this tough work.

CHAPTER NINETEEN
Daddy Day

It had been two months since Steve died. I hurt on a level that was so deep, I had no idea how I was going to get through the pain. I knew I couldn't make it through life being that miserable. I knew God wanted me to find a way to get through my pain, to heal, to grow, and to give back by helping others, but at the time, that seemed impossible.

I struggled with the fact that Steve worked so hard in life, trying to do the right thing for so many people — and then poof, in a moment he was gone, his life was over. How could that be? I ached when I thought of him being forgotten, his own daughter, Makena, not even getting to know who he was, what he loved, how he laughed, what he wanted for her, and all the plans he had to show her the world, to teach her about God. The list was endless. But now he was gone. How could I share Steve and everything he loved and stood for with our little women? How were we supposed to work our way through the pain of letting go and moving on, yet not forget about him? It broke my heart to think of Makena not getting to know her daddy, for Amanda and Sara to feel abandoned again, and for all the things that Steve stood for to disappear.

I prayed that God would show me how to let go of Steve, get through the grief, and somehow begin a new life. Once again it became clear to me that the answer was to make friends with grief — to get to know her, to listen to her, to accept her, to trust her, to welcome her into my life. If I was able to do it, accept Steve's death and do the work of grieving his loss, would the pain go away? I was willing to give it a try even though I didn't know what that meant.

Death is the one thing that doesn't get easier or better as time goes by. It's just the opposite. The more time that passes, the worse it gets because your brain starts to grasp the fact that the person you loved is not coming back. For a while, you can convince yourself that they're on a long trip or a great vacation or anything that helps you pretend they're not gone forever. But then time makes you get real and face the fact that the person you loved, the person you thought you were going to spend forever with, is dead. It's too final to even comprehend.

Grief felt like a battle between my heart and mind. My mind wanted to deal with the truth, move on, and find something or someone that would make me feel good again. My heart said, *No way. You can't forget someone you loved, someone that devoted his life to you — your children's father. Please don't forget him.* "Dear God," I prayed, "how do I do this? How do I make peace with my mind and heart? How do I honor Steve and his life and yet give us the freedom to create a new life? I want his joy and love of life to live on forever. I want our girls to know him—the things he loved, the things that brought him joy, inspired him, challenged him, what helped him to become the man I knew. I want to celebrate Steve's life, his love, his legacy, and his passions. How do I do this, dear God?"

In a very quiet whisper, God gave me Daddy Day as his answer to that prayer. I didn't know what Daddy Day was, but it felt right and I wanted to figure it out. So as a family, on the 28th of every month, the day Steve completed his life on earth and began his new life with Jesus, we celebrate Steve's life. We call this Daddy Day. We spend the day sharing stories about Steve, laughing, crying, whatever the day brings. We also do something special for our hearts because that's what Steve would do for us if he were here. We come up with something fun to do that brings a smile to our lives, just as Steve did. Every Daddy Day is different, just the way Steve would have wanted it because he loved variety. But every month on the 28th, our hearts get to remember the man that changed our lives.

During the first six months of Daddy Days, we spent most of them crying. It was the one day we all let down and felt sad together. At first I thought it was a stupid idea, torturing us with memories every month. I was afraid my little women were going to hate Daddy Day and me for making them hurt so much with all the memories. I asked them to write Steve a letter each month on Daddy Day just to share how they were feeling. I thought since we started our life with Steve by him writing me love letters that maybe we would begin to heal by writing him love letters.

As much as it all hurt, by the end of the day when we were cooking his favorite meal or going out to In-N-Out Burger, one of his favorite places, we would be laughing. We would share a funny memory or something silly that he used to do. Our eyes would be so puffy from all our crying that we would just look at each other and laugh. We would hug each other so tight because we wanted to make sure that we were all going to be together forever, because it just hurt too much. Month by month, Daddy Day became our favorite day, just because it was our day to be together as a family. Wasn't it just like God to take something awful like death and give us a gift of life through it? We serve such an amazing God, and for this I give thanks.

On the first anniversary of Steve's death, July 28, 2005, I decided that since Steve loved to read, every Daddy Day I would give each daughter a book, kind of like our own little Daddy Day Book Club. I gave them a book based on what Steve would have been teaching them about life if he were here. I wanted them to feel Steve's love for them and offer words of advice, just like what he would be doing if he were alive. It could be his gift to them — the love of reading, the wisdom of great words, and the adventure of wonderful writings. And so our Daddy Day Book Club began.

We did our best to find hope, one Daddy Day at a time.

CHAPTER TWENTY
Too Much Pain

The months were slowly passing by, and it was September now. Amanda and Sara had gone back to college. Makena thought it was normal to wake up with a construction crew telling her good morning and pancakes from McDonalds for breakfast. I would drop her off at kindergarten and spend the day going through the motions of whatever needed to be done. God and I had many conversations about "how" — *Please, dear God, tell me, show me, anything to make the pain go away.*

Little did I know that Sara was giving up hope. The grief, the pain was just too much for her. She had so many feelings of guilt and shame about Steve dying that she was searching for anything to make the pain stop. All the unresolved issues of abandonment and anger took over with a vengeance. She was at college but had stopped going to class and started using drugs to make it through the day. I didn't know what was going on, and if I had known, I'm not sure what I would have done anyway. I had nothing left in me to help her, or so I thought.

It was late in the afternoon, and I got a call from Sara. She needed to talk to me. *Please God, help me, I can't take any more bad news.* She came home, shaking and looking like death herself — who knew how long she had been fading away. She sat next to me, crying, and through her tears she shared with me that she wanted to die. She sobbed about how much it hurt and how sorry she was that Steve had died. I don't remember all her words or how long we sat together, but these words — "Mom, I just wanted you to find me" — pierced my soul. At that moment, I found her — thank you, God! I wasn't sure what to do next, but I knew I was going to find help and get her well. And so, once again, God and I started talking about what he wanted me to do. I listened. I was too broken myself to have any thoughts or opinions about how to get through any of it. I had surrendered everything to him, and now he could show me how to love my daughters like he wanted them to be loved.

I called Gary, a counseling friend, and he directed me to a drug rehabilitation center. Together, both terrified of what lay ahead, we went and checked her in. It was a thirty-day program, and I wouldn't be able to see or talk to her during that time. *Really, God? This is going to help?* We held each other. We cried. We both wanted to run out of that place as fast as we could, but we both knew we didn't even know where we would run to. I pealed Sara off of me, and without looking back, I walked out of that place. I drove my car around the block, parked, and sobbed. *Dear God, you must help me and my little women. We are so lost and broken.*

It was time to pick Makena up from kindergarten, and the contractors had called, needing me to choose a paint color. And so the days went by like that. The rehab center had made an exception for Sara and me to see each other since her dad had just died. They allowed me to sit in the lobby, and when she passed by, going to her class or to her meals, I could give her a hug. I would sit there for hours just waiting for that moment when she, with all the other people, would walk by in single file. We would cling to each other. We would cry, and then she would keep walking. Everything about that month was awful. Steve would have been so good at handling it. He would have known just what to do. The only experience I had with drug addiction was with Sara's biological father — and the drugs had won that battle. *Dear God, please don't let me lose Sara to addiction.*

Parent Day. Oh great — time to spend a weekend with other parents, hearing all about why our children were drug addicts, what role we had played, and what we were supposed to do when they finished their program the following week. I have to tell you, I had nothing left in me. So God and I sat in that room, listening to sad stories about lives that had been ruined by addiction. Lots of emotions, lots of tears, lots of pain, but a bit of hope. I hoped that Sara was facing all the demons she had tried to pretend didn't exist. I hoped that she had found a way to make peace with the tough stuff that had made up the chapters of her life story. I was sorry that things had turned out the way they had, but I knew God had a plan and she and I just had to ask him what he wanted us to do, moment by moment, day by day. And so we did.

Sara got to come home a few days before her twentieth birthday. As tough as it was to take her to rehab, picking her up was scary too. I didn't know what to do to support her. All of her friends were drug addicts, so

I didn't want her reconnecting with them. She had lived away from home, and now she was moving back in with me and Makena to a home under construction. They didn't recommend her getting a job right away because she needed time to go to meetings. She needed structure and counseling. The list went on and on of all the things that had to happen to make sure she didn't relapse. Again. . . *Really, God? You think I can handle this along with everything else?*

CHAPTER TWENTY-ONE
Remodel of a Lifetime

The days were passing, but the pain wasn't going away. I did what I needed to do for the contractors and for my little women, and when I found a moment for myself, I wrote to Steve. It was by taking pen to paper and writing to him that my need to communicate subsided. The power of something so simple — yet the permanence it creates — documented our love forever.

Hi Babe,

We got the kitchen countertops installed tonight. Everyone says how beautiful they look. . .I look at them and see you and me discussing them. I can't believe you are not here. It just feels so wrong to have this house coming together just like we had planned, yet you are not here. Amanda, Makena, and I were checking out our new kitchen, and I asked them what they thought. . .Amanda said that you would have loved it, and Makena said, "He does love it! He can see it from heaven!" Oh, to have such a pure heart. I too know that you can see it, but oh how I wish you were here to see it with me.

John was here taking the final measurements for your library. Wow, it is going to be incredible. Finally a place for all your books. Oh I can just see you arranging them and admiring them and so pleased that you finally have a place for all of them. I smile as I think of that, and then I think of me trying to arrange them and tears fall on my checks. I wanted to get a library ladder, but it was way out of our budget. I could see you smiling at me as I told you I wanted it, but you looking at John and without a word letting him know not to include the ladder in the bid. I didn't get the ladder. . .

And then there is Makena's room, oh my goodness…

I chuckle every time I see it. I think of what you would be saying or even if she would have such a room. So this is how I think the story would have gone if you were here. . .I would have told you my idea, to have a bunk bed made that looks like a playhouse. The bottom of the house could be her play area, and her bed would be like a top bunk. It would not be that big of a deal. I would of course share this idea with you as we sipped our wine and talked about our many ideas for the house. You would not have commented on my idea; instead you would have moved on to another subject, hoping that I would not bring such a concept up again. I would know exactly what you were doing and would move on with the conversation with you. We would enjoy another glass of wine, and I would bring it up again. You would agree that it would be cute and fun but not something we needed to pursue. Enter Makena. . .she would tell you all about how she wanted a pink playhouse with a princess bed on top. She would do a much better job telling you all her great ideas, each one involving the color pink. You would lift her up onto your lap, give her a big hug, and hope that she too would forget such a concept. The two of you would converse a while, and you would try to wrap up the conversation with another big hug and reassure her that she did not need a pink playhouse bed. She would look into your eyes and with all her charm tell you quite the contrary. You would snuggle up with her and say, "Do you really want a pink playhouse bed?" She would say, "Oh yes, Daddy, please can I have one?" and you would give her a big hug and say, "Why not."

So, knowing all of this, I hired a guy to build her a playhouse bed. He took the measurements, and it seemed like a simple project. Weeks later, he showed up to assemble the playhouse bed. Once it was complete, it was huge, it was too big for the room. I don't know what happened to his measurements. The mattress would not fit upstairs as planed without Makena only having a few inches between her and the ceiling. So, calmly I proposed building her a bed in her closet area. And then building her a smaller closet in another part of the room. Months later, Makena has a two story, pink playhouse in her room, a new bed built in her closet, and a very small new closet. Of course, she wanted pink chandeliers for her lights. . .she has your taste, my dear. It is a dream room, one that she loves, and as much as it is way over the top, it seems a bit irrelevant in the scope of things.

As for Amanda, she chose to have a pink room too. Pretty pink carpet and light rose walls, it makes you smile just walking in.

Sara has not started designing her room yet. I can see you cringing at the thought of what shade of black she is going to paint all of the walls. As we know, she will spend endless hours designing and decorating and then go off to college again. Of course we won't be able to touch the room, and no one else truly enjoys a room done in black and white quite the way Sara does.

It is such an odd feeling, watching this house transform from our vision to reality. It has been such a long journey that I only have unfamiliar memories. Vivid pictures of us together in this house, yet I feel so lost.

We should be admiring the new kitchen, sipping on wine, and chatting endlessly about all the details of the construction. Instead, I just gaze at it, a bit detached, afraid I will fall apart if I think about it too much. I reach for the phone to call a friend to come over and have a glass of wine with me, but you were my best friend. It is you I want to share this moment with.

I push back the tears and continue my night. I read Makena her bedtime stories. We say her prayers, which always includes saying hi to you and making a few requests of things we hope you and God will do for us. I give her a kiss and miss you!

With all my love,
C

CHAPTER TWENTY-TWO
Touching the Pain

As time went on without Steve, I became so aware of the simple things in life that seemed so ordinary yet left such a longing in my soul. It was death that awakened me to my life.

The pain of Steve's death taught me the value of love and its amazing healing powers. When I let go of my fear of touching the pain of grief and instead accepted it, I began to heal. My healing came from feeling the vulnerability of being alone and just relying on love to get me through it. It was not a kind of love I had ever known; it was a love that started with faith, continued with hope, and grew as I trusted the love I felt from so many different people.

Along the way, I continued to find some relief from the pain by writing love notes to Steve. . .

Hi Babe,

I miss you.

I miss that we will never look across the room, catch each other's eyes, and smile because we have each other.

I miss being your wife.

I miss being loved by you.

I miss that I don't get to share tomorrow with you.

I miss taking your hand and instantly knowing where I am going.

I miss the simple things, our nightly glass of wine, our tender kisses, and our passion for our dreams.

I am so sorry that I stopped dreaming because life got so tough, that I gave up, that I gave in to doubt and fear.

I am so sorry that our daughters don't get to have a daddy to love them, to hold them, and to protect them.

I am so sorry that you had to put so much time into working on projects that were not worthy of your time just because we needed the money.

I am so sorry that I cared about what the world thought and spent so much time, energy, and resources trying to make it all make sense.

I wish that I would have asked you if you were scared.

I wonder what we would have done differently if we would have talked about this night...

The nights that we spend separated, you with God and me with our family.

What is it that you wanted to tell me?

I think that we did not talk about it because it was too hard, too much to even try to bear to think about — to plan to be apart.

From the moment you declared your love to me, I have not been alone; you have cared for me, you have nurtured me, you have suffered because of me, and you have truly loved me.

How did this happen?

How does it work that you give up so much to love me and then must leave so I get a glimpse of what your love has done for me?

Oh, you have left me with an ache that vibrates my very soul, but amazingly enough, you have left me with great hope. I long for the day to be with you again. The day I get to smile again and not be holding back my tears.

Oh, how I miss you ...

With all my love,

C

CHAPTER TWENTY-THREE
I Love You, Steve

Sara had been out of the drug rehab center for one month. We were muddling through every minute of every day—not gracefully, just merely making it through. Both of us were totally unsure of what to do next. We found it difficult to communicate with each other because we both hurt too much. We were afraid that if we said anything, maybe it would be those words that would put one of us over the edge. We were both living so close to it. We couldn't handle any more loss; we just needed love. Because we were too fragile to talk about how we were feeling, Sara turned to her journal to find a safe place to touch her feelings and maybe make peace with all the broken pieces of her shattered life. The following is one of the journal entries she wanted to share with you.

> Dear Journal,
>
> Well it's like 8:20 pm and I have had a good day. Today is the 4-month anniversary of my dad's death, and I am doing okay. Yesterday was a terrible day for me. I had lost all hope and was miserably depressed about all of life. But that was yesterday, and today I am happy. Today was probably so good because the past two days have been so awful.
>
> If I could have, the past two days I would have been messed up, wasted out of my mind. Lately I have been having such strong, overpowering thoughts of drinking. I have wanted a beer, obsessive thoughts and cravings since Thanksgiving. Today was the first day I was lifted from those thoughts. Today I went to church and they said that people spend so much time looking, searching for happiness and if they would stop searching for it and just live life and keep busy, happiness would find them. I need to take that advice. Stop looking for happiness! Get motivated, be productive, accomplish as much as possible each day and happiness will come.
>
> I am happy because today God kept me sober. Today I have 23 days of sobriety! I have a house with my own bed to sleep in. I have a mom who loves me so much. Today I was in a good mood all day. Thanks to the Lord who lifted me from Satan's grasp from previous days. You know, 4 months ago today, I thought I would never survive. When my dad died, I never thought tomorrow would come. I was hopeless and in great sorrow.

I physically could not stand. My emotions were so overpowering there was no way I was ever going to make it. But here I sit exactly 4 months later alive. Somehow I survived. And I survived long enough to have a wonderful day only 4 months after I thought it would impossible to ever have a wonderful day again.

Because every second of your love comes and goes. To me, the world seemed as if it would never go on, but it did. Time never stops or slows down or changes. It is constant. You have no control over it. Life went on after Steve died, the end of the world did not occur, and I survived.

I am such a better person today than I was only 4 months ago. I have changed so much. Everything I knew, everything I had, changed, the people I loved and looked up to—gone. My dad, Mallory, college, my apartment, all my friends and way of life … gone. That's so many holes, so many pieces of me that I lost, but look at me now. I'm so different, I can't wait to see what the next 4 months of my life will bring. Good days, bad days. That's a given. But the thing I have learned the most is I will survive! What doesn't kill you will make you stronger!

Before, honestly in my heart, I truly believed I would not make it through Steve dying. I said out loud and believed in my heart, "I cannot handle it, I will not make it, and I cannot do this." I think I truly thought I was going to die too. Grief was too overpowering for me. There was just too much. But now those feelings of total despair have been lifted from me. And I know that I am going to face hard things and life will not be easy, but the Lord Jesus Christ promises me I will make it. He says he will never give me anything I can't handle. He will give me the strength I need to get through every situation, I just have to trust Him and today I believe that. In my heart there is hope for tomorrow. I know it will come, it always does whether we want it to or not.

Thank you, Lord, for my dad and for putting him in my life. And help me to keep him in my heart.

Love, Sara

I love you, Steve.

CHAPTER TWENTY-FOUR
Love Hurts

December 2, 2004, my fortieth birthday. Steve and I had made reservations to spend a night at Post Ranch Inn, my favorite place in the world. We had never spent the night there because it was so expensive. Instead, we would have a glass of wine on the patio and dinner at sunset. It was my place. It defined love for me. And we were going to spend my birthday there — but not anymore.

Hi Babe,

Well, you died before my birthday. I buried you in the closest cemetery to Post Ranch Inn. So, this is my first trip back to see you since I buried you here.

I checked into my room at Post Ranch Inn. Waiting for me were many bottles of wine — every one of my girlfriends had sent one because they were so worried about me being here without you. I needed a lot more than many bottles of wine to make it through not being with you.

I had dinner on my birthday, alone, at a table for one. Just behind me was the table that we shared a meal with our family just months before. I sat at a quiet table, no conversation. Months earlier we sat at a crowded table, constant conversation, the girls putting up with us as we chatted about all of our wonderful memories here at my favorite spot. Wow, I can't believe those moments in time are gone forever. I can feel them. I can taste them. I can see them. I just can't have them anymore!

Dec. 3, 2004

I spent the afternoon in Carmel looking for the perfect piece of art that would remind me of us and our times here on the beach. I looked in gallery after gallery — and nothing. Nothing that said, "I love you with all my heart. I will leave you soon, but always remember this spot. Remember my touch as I reached for your hand. Remember my kiss as I promised you forever. Remember all of our moments, for they have led us to today. I'm so sorry I have had to go, but I leave you with the intense sound of our love thundering onto the sandy beaches below the majestic cliffs. For when the sun sets, I still love you. And when the view is dark, hidden from the light, I am still here, loving you, caring for you and holding you. And when you must leave the beach, I will go with you, for now I can always take care of you."

In the last gallery, I saw a painting of a child in bed, the morning sun shining through her window. The light was radiant, and instantly I thought of Makena on the day you died. I thought of how bright her world had been and then how one morning as she awakened, it appeared to be another beautiful day, and yet it was the day you died.

I can still see the two of you together. You were lying in bed very ill, and she was looking at you wondering where her daddy had gone. We lifted her into your arms; you cradled her and sang your song to her . . .

Why did you have to go? Why did you have to leave us all? I feel as though in our life painting, there is light, there is love, laughter, all in bright colors, and then it is as if the artist puts down the brush, maybe to enjoy a sip of vino, and then without notice — unable to ever pick up the brush again.

Dec. 4, 2004

As I sit here and watch the waves, I think of you. . .

I think of all the waves we tried to ride. Oh the high of catching that perfect wave and riding it in. Oh, baby, that was good! And then there were the crashes. Oh, how they hurt — oh, the broken hearts, the stunning pain of wipe out!

I love you for always going out to catch the waves. The ocean was too rough for me; it broke my spirit, and it hurt too much. But through the years, you loved me. You brought me to the beach every day. You let me watch you, cheer for you, and fall in love with you as you showed me how to love the beach again.

I love you. I am happy for your ticket home, but I miss you. I miss us! Why did forever have to be so short?

I kiss you. I hold you. I send my love with you. I ask that you not forget me, and I will never forget you, my love.

Until we meet again. . .

Dec. 5, 2004

Here I sit in front of your grave. I'm going home today, back to our life. I'm going to try to let go of you and to let go of me being a part of you. I know that you have transitioned to God's other work for you.

Thank you for your love. Thank you for providing for our family. Thank you for being my potter and for shaping my life. First by sharing your life with me. Second by sharing your faith with me. Third by sharing your vision with me, and now by sharing your death with me. It is only by death that we are given life. I know that. I thank Jesus for giving his life for us. Now you, giving your life for our family. I too will give my life for us, for our faith, for our children, for our vision to make the world a better place.

It is very peaceful here at your grave. The birds are chirping away. The sun is shining through a light fog, yet the strong trees seem to cradle all the tenderness that lives here. So many people, so many lives, so many dreams, so many tears. It is interesting that those of us left behind seem to come here to gain life. It is busy here today, many people coming to arrange flowers, say prayers. I don't even know what all is going on, but you can feel the serenity, the peace of letting go yet never forgetting.

I like Monterey, strangely enough. It feels like home. We always lived to be a part of something bigger than ourselves and this is where you found a place big enough to feel small. Not small in life but where you belonged, among the vast ocean and the ever reaching Redwoods.

I don't know when I will be back, my dear. I know you know where my heart is, and I pray for our connection to grow stronger by the day and for our time apart to be used to strengthen our walk of faith. I miss you and love you.

Here's to you, babe. I raise my glass: for all the love that you have felt and given away to others; for all the joy and laughter that you have left behind; for all the kisses you have given me; for the things that touched your soul. For the moments in time that now define our life together. For you and me and to wherever we will now go. . .

With all my love,
C

CHAPTER TWENTY-FIVE
The Holidays

They were tough times — all the firsts without Steve. I don't remember Thanksgiving, but I knew I couldn't skip Christmas. I was focused on getting the house finished enough so that we wouldn't have to spend Christmas with the contractors. I wanted the house to feel like a home during the holidays.

The morning of December 24th was busy. We had so many contractors at the house finishing up. By 2:00 everyone was leaving, and the girls and I were left alone for the first time in our remolded home. All the ladders were packed up, the tool boxes were removed from the middle of the floor, layers of dust were gone, and windows had been cleaned. It was beautiful — and quiet. It was eerie to see the house finally look like what Steve and I had drawn up on paper.

The funny part about that day was that I hadn't thought about ordering furniture. Steve and I had given away all of our furniture instead of storing it, so when it came time to move back in, I had nothing for us to move. The girls and I decided to go get a Christmas tree. We had plenty of room for it since it was the only thing in the house. We brought in the pool furniture and made ourselves at home.

We started to unpack the Christmas trunks. We always decorated our tree with ornaments that were pictures from every year. It made the Christmas tree feel like a scrapbook, and each picture brought back such fun memories. It was different opening up the ornament boxes this year. The girls looked at me as if to say, *Mom, can we do this?* They always looked at me like that now, and I responded as I had gotten so accustomed to doing — with a hug and *yes, we can do this together.* I made some hot chocolate, put on our Christmas music, and we made our way through the boxes. When it was time to hang the stockings, Makena asked if we should still hang Daddy's stocking. "Of course we should. He's still part of our family," Amanda and Sara said. We were still hanging on to Steve, but Makena was beginning to move on.

I wanted to somehow make Christmas special even though I knew it would be filled with painful memoires. Months earlier, I had been thinking about this day — Christmas morning, without Steve — and had come up with a gift idea for the whole family. I took Steve's clothes to a quilt maker, and she made quilts from Steve's shirts and jeans for each one of us. We spent the day all snuggled up in our Daddy Quilts. Every patch was so familiar, I could see Steve wearing those shirts and jeans, but now we just had to wrap ourselves up in his love.

I had a special box in my stocking Christmas morning too. I had taken Steve's wedding ring to a jeweler and had it made into a cross necklace for me. It was beautiful. The girls loved it too; it was symbolic to us all, a family treasure. I wasn't sure when I would be ready to take off my wedding ring, but I knew that time would come, and when it did, I would know what to do with that ring as well.

Someone sent this Christmas poem to us, and I love it:

"My First Christmas in Heaven"

I see the countless Christmas trees around the world below with tiny lights, like Heaven's stars, reflecting on the snow.

The sight is so spectacular; please wipe away the tears, for I am spending Christmas with Jesus Christ this year.

I hear the many Christmas songs that people hold so dear, but the sound of music can't compare with the Christmas choir up here.

I have no words to tell you, the joy their voices bring, for it is beyond description, to hear the angels sing.

I know how much you miss me, I see the pain in your heart, but I'm not so far away, we really aren't apart.

I send you each a special gift, from my heavenly home above. I send you each a memory of my undying love.

After all, love is a gift more precious than pure gold. It was always most important in the stories Jesus told.

Please love and keep each other, as my Father said to do, for I can't count the blessings or love He has for each of you.

So have a Merry Christmas and wipe away that tear, remember I'm spending Christmas with Jesus Christ this year.

Unknown Author

CHAPTER TWENTY-SIX
Only By the Grace of God

As the last boxes of Christmas were packed away, our family was left to face the New Year. As painful as Christmas was, it was a distraction from the "what next" in our lives. We were so lost. We all hated our lives. No matter what spin we tried to put on it, we couldn't find a simple thread to hang onto that even mattered to us. We pretended to be okay, not for our own sake but just for the sake of not messing up the family any more than it already was.

There was no way we were going to bring in the New Year without some sort of plan about what we each wanted to try to do with our lives. I desperately needed to find hope — anything to feel like getting up tomorrow would serve any purpose other than survival. I wanted my little women to find hope, to have a plan, to have a dream, to have anything other than the pain that had moved into our lives. But that was not happening. The more I pushed for a plan, the more Amanda and Sara withdrew. It was too much.

What I thought was showing love was breaking my little women's hearts one more time. My intense desire to try to make life better so it would not hurt them so much was causing them more pain. Why couldn't I just hold them and let them know that I too was broken into a million pieces? I couldn't. I was afraid if I went there, the pain would be too much.

As Sara was withdrawing from me and the family, she was desperate to try to stay sober, so she would snuggle up on her bed in her black bedroom and share her heart with a blank piece of paper. Her journal became the only friend she had. The following is another journal entry she's chosen to share with you.

Dear Journal,

Only by the grace of God did I get through today. Today I was so close to losing my sobriety. I actually went to get the bottle of vodka out of the kitchen cabinet. As I was reaching for it, a construction worker walked in the front door. I was so scared it was my mom, I closed the cabinet immediately! At that moment I was too scared to take the little bottle of vodka. I felt like God was standing over me and had the worker walk into the room just right at that moment to slow my thoughts and keep me sober.

Still I took it, but it made me think twice before drinking it. Actually I did not drink it.

  Today was terrible for me. It was just a carryover from yesterday's awfulness. My mom kills me. She makes me hate myself. She says things that hurt me. She gets so mad at me, and I feel like all I do is screw up her life. Really that is all I do. Amanda and I mess up her perfect world. I am really just a screw up. Everything I do is always wrong. I always make her so unhappy. I bet she would be a lot happier if I would have died instead of Steve. I know she would be. At least they had love. According to my mom, I have no love and I let no one love me. It is so important to her for me to find true happiness. Real love. To find who the real Sara is. Who cares! She gets so caught up in fixing me all the time, always working on trying to make me better. She says she doesn't know who I am, she doesn't know her own daughter. . .I need to tell her who I am. She makes it such a big deal. She makes me not even know who I am. She does the same thing to Amanda. She yells, "Who are you? Who is Amanda?" Amanda says, "I don't know." Then Mom says, "You need to figure that out." I listen to her say this to Amanda and then she says the same thing to me. Well, Mom, this is me. I have no earth-shattering answer to that question. My mom is very firm and strong on her opinions and beliefs. She can sit down and say, "Hi, I'm Carlette, I am a mom, I like Mexican food, Dr. Pepper, Godiva chocolate, my favorite color is purple, I love hearts, and God is the sole basis of my life."

  Me, my name is Sara. I am a vegetarian. I don't have a favorite soda; I'll drink any of them, sometimes none. It doesn't really matter where we eat, I don't really love any restaurant, my favorite color is black, but I like rainbow things just as well. I look the best in pink. I love music, I don't really have a favorite, and it just depends on the day and event. I hate animals. I think they are gross and annoying. I love to exercise, kind of obsessively. I'll play any sport or workout with anyone. I like to drink alcohol. I love to get wasted and go to clubs and dance all night. I don't like to dance with boys. I'd rather dance on stage or a table, or with my friends. Guys/girls, just not with people I don't know. I love the feeling of ecstasy. It is the best feeling in the entire world. A good pill that is. I also love Adderall. More than anything, but I don't like to be messed up. I hate it actually. I don't really like coke, and I hate smoking weed, but I do them both. I do not like to drink unless I have Adderall, because I hate how you get so tired when you're drunk. I don't watch TV or like the computer. I don't really even like talking on the phone. I hate being alone. I hate being bored. I am a funny person, I always make people laugh. I'm outgoing and I do lots of random things. I am creative and artsy, a little untraditional in my choice of style. I do all the things people talk about doing and never do. It's my greatest strength and my biggest weakness. I have friends who are 14 and 35. I'll dye my hair, get tattoo piercing without thinking twice. There is nothing in life I think I can't do, or really won't do. I am good at everything but the very best at nothing, because I don't ever stick to the same thing long enough to become the best. I jump 100% into things right away. All or nothing. Go big or go home. And then I'm done. Time for something new. And with that, there is no stability in my life.

I am 20 years old! I am not supposed to have some career and life-long plan. But that's how my mom treats me. There is no living in the moment with her. Just doing day-to-day things. There's always got to be this big reason, this soul searching answer. She always tells me how unhappy I am, and how I can't go on like this. I have got to find happiness. I am not unhappy with my life. She is. She has these visions for me that I don't have. She wants this life for me full of love and happiness. I know exactly what she wants. She wants me to find the perfect guy, is what it really comes down to. She thinks no guy has ever treated me well. None of my boyfriends are ever good enough, and I like to live with pain and heartache, and she always says, "Why won't you let anyone love you!"

Mom, I can't even stand to be around myself all the time, I don't really love me, in all truth you don't really love me either. According to you, you don't even know me, how can you love somebody you don't know? I am your blood and daughter. I am half of you, you had me, your love is for your daughter, it wouldn't matter who it was me or any other girl, that love is only based on the fact that I happen to be your daughter. Your love is not for me. The Sara you want so desperately to know and figure out you wouldn't love, and that's me.

Stop trying to fix me. . .just accept me. . .you have to accept me before you can love me. . .

Love,
Sara

CHAPTER TWENTY-SEVEN
Getting Real. . .Real Pearls

And so the story goes. . .

There once was a little girl whose daddy gave her a beautiful pearl necklace. Oh how she loved the necklace. She wore it every day with great pride. During the day, when she was happy, she twirled her fingers through it as she giggled and enjoyed the fun of the moment. At night when she was tired and winding down to go to sleep, her little fingers touched the pearls as a gentle reminder of how much her daddy loved her. She had no idea that they were fake pearls; to her, they were the most precious gems she had ever owned or would ever want to own. They meant everything to her.

Years passed, and the little girl was becoming a young lady. Her daddy sat her down and said it was time for her to give up her pearl necklace. She was devastated. Why would her daddy demand something so terrible? Why would he take away something that meant so much to her? He told her she could take as long as she needed to say good-bye to her pearl necklace, and when she was ready, to bring it to him. He told her that it was important for her to know that when she gave the necklace back to him, she would never get it back.

The day came, and holding the pearls tightly, she extended her hand to her daddy. She still could not imagine why he would make her do something so painful, but her love for her daddy was more than her love for her pearls. She cried as she opened her clinched hand, and with great sadness, she gave her daddy her pearls.

Her daddy gave her a big hug and handed her a gift. He said that she had not been ready for this gift until she was able to give up her childhood gift. With anticipation, the young lady opened the gift. It was a beautiful pearl necklace. Confused, she looked at her daddy. He explained that this one was a real pearl necklace. He couldn't give it to her until she was ready to let go of the fake one.

I love this story, such a powerful image of God's love for us. In my life, I have hung on to way too many fake pearls. Grief showed me what real pearls are like. They're strong, they're beautiful, and yet they need the sand grinding against them to make them into what they're meant to be. I could feel the sand of life grinding away at our family, and it hurt. We cried. We tried to give up. But God never let us. He loves us too much.

Sometimes I could feel how tightly I was holding on to the life Steve and I had. It was a combination of real and fake pearls. God didn't want my life to have any more fake pearls in it. He wanted me to be able to give up the fake life and trust him. It was tough to do, but I knew the difference now, and I prayed for the courage and strength to let go of my fake pearl life and open my heart to a life of real pearls.

CHAPTER TWENTY-EIGHT
Good-Bye, USA
Hello, South Africa

Sara was lost after coming home from drug rehab. They wanted her to spend her days going to meetings, standing up, saying her name, and announcing that she was a drug addict. Oh no, I knew this was not what God wanted her doing with her life. I knew she was not a drug addict, but that she had made some very bad choices and had paid the price for those choices. It was time to have life be about serving others, not her past. I told her to spend time with God and ask him what he wanted her to do this year, for his glory.

Much to my huge surprise, she told me she wanted to go to Africa. Steve and I were involved in an International Sports Ministry, and I knew of one in South Africa, so I contacted them and asked if Sara could apply to be involved in their ministry. Here is what she wrote for her application letter, detailing why they should accept her into their ministry:

I believe the Lord has a specific plan for my life. I know He has been watching out for me and protecting me since long before I was born. He has wrapped his loving arms around me and spared my life more than once.

My family has always believed in God, and I have been raised in a home where God's rules are the rules we live by. The Lord has always provided for my family everything we have needed, not exactly everything I have thought I needed or wanted though.

Growing up, I never liked school. I felt like I did not fit in anywhere. From the fifth grade until the eleventh grade, I went to a different school every year. I just did not fit in anywhere. In eight grade, I went to a private school and found the "wrong crowd" to hang out with. I began to act out in class and started to get into trouble regularly. At this time in my life, both my parents were working full-time and my mom was pregnant. So, this is when I fell away from the Lord. I had so much anger and hate in my heart, I could not find happiness anywhere. This was my life until the tenth grade when I got kicked out of high school for using drugs. In the tenth grade, I had to move from Phoenix, Arizona, to live with my aunt, uncle, and three cousins in Artesia, New Mexico. Here I strayed from the Lord even more. This year of my life was filled with jealousy, hatred, and so much anger. I was self-medicating myself to stop all these feelings, so I could just relax, fit in, and be cool.

During the summer, I went back to Phoenix to visit my family. While I was there, I got in a very serious car accident. My car was totaled and I was hospitalized. I had broken my pelvic bone three times and my tail bone twice. The firemen did not think I was going to make it. God was there with me the whole time protecting me even though I had stopped praying to Him.

I was in the hospital for two weeks and spent the next three months in a wheelchair. That alone is a miracle, because the doctor said it would be at least a year until I could walk and my parents should hold me back in school. Not only did I walk, but I also started in the first game in my junior year basketball season.

God has a plan for me. It is clear He saved my life as a non-believing sixteen-year-old. I know that if I would have died in that car accident, I would not have been in heaven.

I spent the next two years trying my best to follow God's law. I went on mission trips and shared my testimony with many people. I spoke to a group of about forty youth, and they all accepted Jesus as their savior at the end of my testimony. God was in my heart and He used my life to bring others to know Him. God has a plan for my life that only He knows. I just have to keep my thoughts focused on His will and try every day to be more like Him.

Good-bye, USA! Hello, South Africa!

Sara packed her bags and went to spend a year with the organization called SCAS, Sports for Christ Action South Africa. They have a program called Service Year for Christ. SCAS is a sports ministry, using sports and adventure to share the gospel in schools, by working for and with churches and communities. SCAS is located near Cape Town in the town of Stellenbosch.

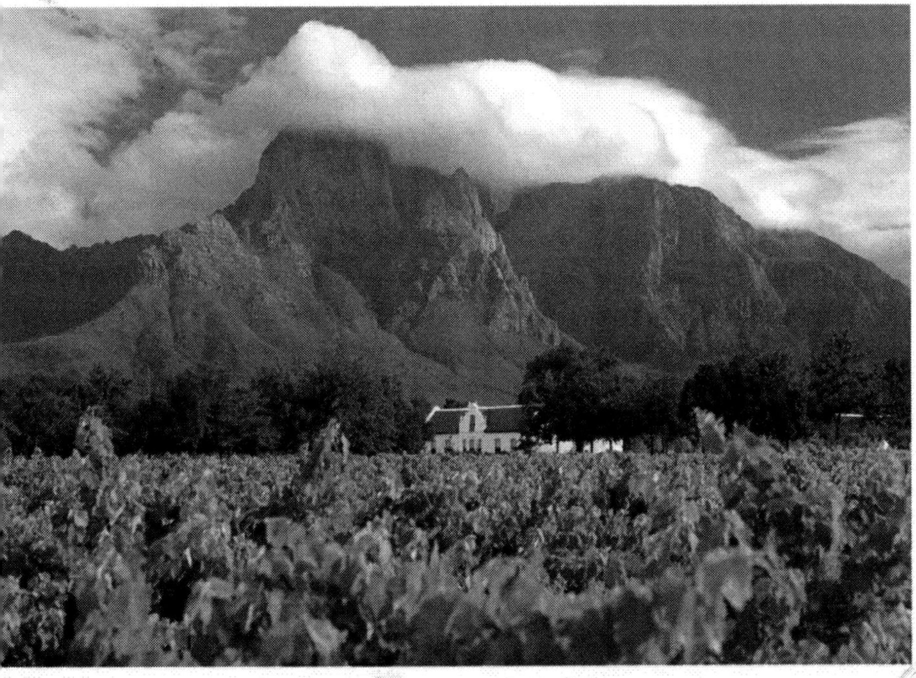

CAPE WINELANDS · SOUTH AFRICA

Hi Mom —
Africa is so Prety. I
thought of Steve there.
It is a Huge wine country
I ate the biggest grapes In
the whole world. I hope
everything Is going good
In America. It is a very
different life out here. But
a good one. I have made good
friends and I am learning
so much! I Love You, and
miss you and Makenna and Amanda.
Tell every one hello for me ♥ Sara

POST CARD POSKAART
ART PUBLISHERS
COPYRIGHT

Carlette Patterson
[illegible]
[illegible]
USA

ART PUBLISHERS (PTY) LTD. DURBAN · JOHANNESBURG · CAPE TOWN

WINELANDS · CAPE PROVINCE · SOUTH AFRICA
... house ... of a mountainous backdrop in this glorious and productive region of the

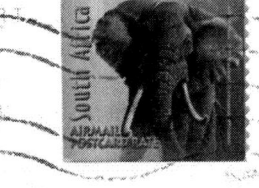

CHAPTER TWENTY-NINE
Hi, Mom, It's Me!

Hi, Mom, it's me! These became precious words to me the year Sara spent in South Africa. I prayed for God to be with her, to protect her, to love her, to heal her, and to please give me the strength to make it through the year.

Our only form of communication was e-mail, and that was only when she was in a town that had an Internet café. I had no idea when we would connect. I would be at my computer early in the morning, and on very special days an e-mail would come through that said, "Hi, Mom, are you there?" I lived for those words. We would then frantically write back and forth until her time on the computer ran out of money based on the few coins she had in her pocket.

Fri 1/14/2005 7:43 AM
Hi Mom!

Hello from South Africa! Today is the first day we got to go to town, so I could not type any day but Fridays. Everything is awesome here. I am having such a great time. All the people are so nice and I really fit right in except I don't speak Africans.

They all speak pretty good English and I have some interpreters. It is so different than I thought it would be, but a lot better. All the sports they play I have never even watched. No one here even has a basketball or a hoop. I have played hockey, thrown a rugby ball for the first time, and played cricket. I am learning so many new sports. We hiked a huge mountain with the best view. It took a few hours and sometimes it was scary, but the view of South Africa was worth it. We sang praise songs and I could really feel the Lord up there. It was awesome.

Oh yeah, as one of our "get in shape" things, we had to push a van around this track ten times. A van! Only in Africa do they push vans for fun. Everyone is in very good shape and we work out all the time. I really love it. They know I am a vegetarian, so they make me special food. Don't worry, I am not starving. Different food, but no meat.

The outreach we are going to do is incredible. The people here have serious spiritual gifts. It is serious ministry we are doing. So much prayer

— we pray out loud for 30 minutes. It is all so amazing. It is very different than America but much better.

Everyone loves me because I am an American. They make me say things in their language and then they all laugh, it is great. Well, I just wanted to say hi and tell you that it's going so well. I am so glad — times 100 — that I came. I love you. Tell Amanda and Makena I said hi. I will talk to you later. I love you.

Sara

Sat 1/22/2005 5:01 AM
Hi Mom,

Greetings from South Africa. Well we got to go to the mall twice this week. Awesome. Things are going so well still. We have great speakers and pastors, and I feel so inspired to save the world. Can you believe the pastor that laid hands on me — he was so amazing. I had not believed him all week. He kept telling us these far out stories and how powerful God and the Holy Spirit was. I would just give him the look like he was crazy. My friend Bennie had been praying every day that something dramatic would happen to me to make me believe. At the end of the week, everyone I was praying with kept telling me this year is going to change my life — amazing things are going to happen to me. I'm like — okay. The pastor was praying for the group and he asked, if you want to change your life — if the Lord is calling you, pulling on your heart to make a difference — come forward and receive the Holy Spirit — you can do miracles and change your life. You know me, I do not go forward on those things, but I felt like I had to, like God was dragging me up there, so I went.

I was in line. I was so scared. I was sure I was going to pass out. I was having such panic and anxiety, so I just started praying. There were four guys that could pray for you. I was just fixed on this pastor, and I was praying for him to be the guy to pray for me. I was going to step out of line to make sure he prayed for me, but then I thought if God wants him to pray for me, he will. Bennie was in front of me and the pastor finished praying for this girl and he was walking toward him and out of nowhere, stopped and at that moment another man finished his prayer and Bennie went to him and the pastor motioned for me to come to him. It was crazy. Then he prayed for me — Mom it was awesome, he told me about the past in my life and so many things had happened to me and I had the gift of speaking and writing and I should not be embarrassed or ashamed about anything but to tell people everything. He said I had the gift of discernment and I have always had this gift, but in the past I did not always do the right thing. He said I manipulated people to get what I wanted and I do not ever have to do that again — God will provide. He said that something happened in our house and it caused me great doubt and confusion and that my house was in great confusion as well. He cast it out of me and the family. I was up praying and I was shaking and he said I suffered from anxiety and he cast it out of me and I no longer was shaking. He said God had blessed me so much and I need to use my blessings to please Him. I opened my eyes and he looked at me and said he sees that I need to practice thanksgiving. That I am not thankful enough for things and I need to start being thankful for everything and just say thank you all the time. Can you believe all that?

Then I was telling Bennie what the pastor said and about how in line I prayed to get the pastor and I did. Bennie told me he too was praying to see the pastor and he was so excited that he was going to see him. As he was walking over there, God told him to stop and turn. He saw I was next and then he knew the pastor was the life-changing thing he had been praying for. Amazing. So I believe everything. I believe God can do anything and I can do anything with Him. The Holy Spirit is alive in me and I am going to share it with the world.

Stuff like this is happening to me all the time. I am in such shock and amazement about all the things God can do. Thank you so much for me coming here, God knew I had to come here, it took me coming all the way to South Africa to believe 100 percent. I am so happy.

I hope your week is going well. Tell Makena I said hi and I love her. Just let me know if you want me to pray for anything. I will. I love you so much and thank you for being my Mom. My life is changing, it's amazing. I love you and will type to you next Friday. Okay have a good week.

Sara

Sat 1/22/2005 5:27 AM

I forgot to tell you another thing the pastor said, that God gave me the gift of intelligence and for some reason I have not thought so. That I did not think I was smart. He said God gave me that gift for a reason and I should not shut the door on it. That I am smart and to finish whatever I gave up on. Cool huh, so the Holy Spirit really gave this pastor a huge vision on my whole life, even school. Wow, God is so powerful. I love you and will talk to you later.

Fri 1/28/2005 7:12 AM
Hi Mom,

Happy Friday and Happy Daddy Day!!! Well I hope you had a good week. I had a pretty good one. Today we prayed for the family and for me in Steve's honor, which was a miracle in itself. This is what happened. Today in my quiet time from 7-8am, I wrote my letter to Steve. It was a lot sadder than I thought it would be and a lot longer too, but good to do. Afterward I was sitting in my room on the bed and I was thinking if they ask for prayer requests today I am going to ask them to pray for our family. But only if they ask, does anyone have something we need to pray for — I was not going to volunteer. I really don't know where these thoughts were coming from because they never ask us if we have a prayer request. They usually tell us what we need to pray for, but still I was having these thoughts.

So I went to class like always. Our teacher was this lady, and the topic we were going to study today was prayer. I was like, okay, still nothing was registering in my mind. So she was talking and telling us prayer will be answered and prayer is so powerful and to pray always. She was giving out Bible verses on how to pray and I found myself thinking, I really don't like to pray, it is not really my favorite part, it is hard for me and I am just doubting and drifting in thought.

So we have a break and Wil comes to the front of the room and says he needs eight guys to be bouncers at the Switch Foot concert. Bennie was so excited. I could tell he wanted to go so bad, but twelve guys wanted to do it, so they drew names out of a hat. I had this feeling that Bennie's name would not get drawn. Four names were picked — not his, so I said, Bennie I am going to pray. I prayed — Lord please let Bennie get picked. Please, he wants to go so bad, please let Bennie get picked. Well the next name was his best friend and then three more names — not him. I said in my head, my prayer did not get answered. I turned to Bennie to say — sorry God did not answer my prayer and at that moment a boy named Vossie said, Bennie you can have my spot. So I said nothing and just kept my mouth shut and felt a little strange.

So the lecturer went on and I was thinking more and more negative thoughts—like I was tired of all this God stuff. I could just go home, who cares. We can never be perfect, so why keep trying and failing and having to ask for forgiveness. And just thoughts like that. Well it was the end of the lecture and the lady said we were to spend the last ten minutes in prayer.

Is there anyone with a prayer request? Not something small. A big prayer request. Something that is on your heart and you want us to pray as a group. I was feeling really guilty. I was not raising my hand. Bennie was now sitting next to me, he was saying stuff to me like — lay it before God, bring it before God, come on Sara, God knows. He will bless you if you lay it before Him. Give it to God. And the lady was like, okay anyone at all have something on your heart. I raised my hand and said, "um please pray for me and my family, my dad died six months ago today and it is hard so please pray for us today." I was trying so hard not to cry. I went to the front and everyone prayed. It was awesome!

Afterwards Bennie was like — sorry if I pushed you, but something was telling me not to give up, that you needed to raise your hand. So that was just what I needed to get my mind back on track.

I'll tell you, God has to keep giving me these miracles to keep me on track. I am so thankful for them. Today was a miracle day for me and I hope you are having the same. I know that if I find myself crying and still grieving, so do you. I love you and I am confident that Steve is in heaven with the Lord — what more could we ask for than that! I read a verse in the Bible that really helped me, but I don't remember it offhand, so I will send it to you next week. It is about heaven.

Well that was my day so far, and it is only 4:00. This past week has been good as well. We painted a boys' home and played sports with them. That was really neat. I ate the biggest piece of cake ever, from a coffee shop! People here eat a lot of cake like we eat muffins. So that was cool.

I hope you had a good day. I will pray for your week. I love you and tell Amanda and Makena I said I love them too. Okay, talk to you next Friday. I love you.

Sara

The following is the letter that Sara wrote to Steve on Daddy Day, six months after he died:

Dear Dad,

Today is a beautiful day in South Africa. The rain is pouring down, and I am inside at a table listening to the rain while someone is playing Christian music in the background. What a nice morning. So, today you have been dead for 6 months. Wow. It feels like only yesterday you were dying. It does not feel like a half a year ago, it is still so fresh in my mind. Then another part of me feels like it was so long ago and you were never even really here. I have so many confusing feelings about you. Whenever I talk to someone, I still speak like you are alive and I refer to my parents back home, not just mom. It is so strange how the human mind works. Don't you think so?

Sometimes I think you dying caused me great trauma in my life. Sometimes I am so sad and depressed and I just want to cry. My brain just can't let go of you. And the way you died was horrible. I can't get those sounds and pictures of you out of my mind. I hate you for dying; I hate the way you died! Watching you get so sick and watching death take over your body. That all feels like yesterday, it feels so like yesterday.

When I was in the bathtub, taking a long shower, singing Amazing Grace and praying for the courage to go into your bedroom, I wanted to tell you that I loved you, that I was sorry for hating you and you were really a good dad. I was just singing Amazing Grace trying to get the courage to go into that room. And when I finally did, when I knocked on the door and asked mom if I could come in, she just stared at me in horror, such fear, and said nothing. She just looked at me with those eyes all white, her pupils were so small but her eyes so big. Then Uncle Bob told me I could come in but you had already passed away not even a moment ago. I was too late, one moment too late.

Right now as I sit here and think back on that day, I get the same feelings of sadness. My body is still overtaken with grief of you dying and the way you looked when you were dead. Those thoughts, I can't get rid of them! How cold your body was when I lay next to you. How awful it was when the morning came and took you away — to see your body lying there on your bed empty, with no soul. Those thoughts all feel like yesterday. Those memories still won't leave my head. That day, today, six months ago, will forever be burned into my mind. But the past six months seem to escape my memory. So much has happened to me in six months, but I am stuck in July 28th 2004.

Today I am in South Africa and here I have turned to the Lord. I have been here for three weeks and I have learned so much. Now I believe in God and in miracles, angles and demons. Now I am able to look back on you dying and see things a little differently. It is hard and I can see it, but I am struggling to accept it.

I am studying the Bible. I am studying God's word, His plans, and what this life is all about. I have found Romans 8:18-30. You suffered so much here on earth in your last few months and now you are in heaven. Wow I am so happy for you! You get to be with Jesus in heaven! How could I be sad? God called you home because your work here is over. I really could not see how your work could be finished because in my eyes your life was nowhere close to over. But I cannot see the big picture; it's God's plan, not mine. He is in charge, not me. This is very hard for me to comprehend. I am so self-absorbed and can only see myself and that I am in pain because you left me. But if I actually think about you for once, you are with the Lord, the creator, the master of the entire universe in paradise. How could I not be excited? You won, you did it, you are in heaven. God said, "Well done, my good and faithful servant." So congratulations!

Something else has been on my heart for the past few days. Our purpose here on earth is to save souls, right? To bring people to God and to the Kingdom of heaven, that's our mission, right? What we are here for? Your soul was saved, you went to heaven. A few days ago I had this conviction in my heart, this conviction that you died to save my soul. My soul was so lost; I did not even think I had a soul. The devil ran my life and I was full of sin. When you died, it took me to my end, I hit bottom a lot faster. Things were so messed up, I had to go to rehab where I got clean and sober at 19. Because your death sped up the process! You dying took me really deep, really fast. If you were still alive, I would probably be doing the same things. Living in sin, not caring about anything and doing nothing with my life. Since you died, I hit the bottom and cried out for help. I got help, good help. I am in Africa finding my soul, reaching out for God's grace, all because of you.

When you and Mom went to Greece, you met Cassie, the guy in charge here. When you died, I lost it and Mom started asking if anyone knew of something I could do. SCAS did Mom a favor and let me come here *because you died. And here my life has changed dramatically!*

So the other day, I felt a strong conviction that you died to save my soul. God's plan, not mine. He saw the big picture of me in South Africa seeking Him. I saw the small picture, myself in pain because I lost you. It is truly bizarre how the world is and how life can change so fast. The future is really nothing, there is no such thing. If you asked me last July if I thought you would die and in 6 months I would be in South Africa serving, singing, and praising God, I would tell you that you were crazy. But by God's grace, I am here.

Thank you, Lord, for having a bigger picture than me. I love you, and, Dad, if you did die to save my soul, thank you for that. I won't let you down.

Love,
Sara

CHAPTER THIRTY
My Faith

I marvel at how the chapters of our love story continue to be written. I am amazed at life, how fragile it is, yet how strong I am becoming. To Steve, I thank you for loving me from so far away.

I wondered if this was faith. I felt Steve, yet I couldn't see him. I knew that what we felt for each other was bigger than all the problems the world threw at us. We found strength from somewhere, a gentle knowing that God was caring for us every minute of every day. Was this faith?

We had faith when Steve was alive. I saw faith when Steve took his last breath. I found faith to be stronger than any feeling I had ever known when I had to bury Steve. I now relied on faith to guide me through my days. I knew that faith was more than just a feeling or a word or something unknown, because it became my breath of life that I relied on without fail to see me through another day.

My faith did not die when Steve's life ended. Something about watching him die made my faith so much stronger. It was as if when he took his last breath, I was blessed with more faith because only God knew what lay ahead of me and he was preparing me for all of my tomorrows.

My faith was tested as my time without Steve lengthened. The harsh reality of his absence felt cruel. His simple touch, his calming words, his playful spirit became a distant memory. I felt the presence of loneliness touching my body every minute of every day. And when I wondered if I could take another moment of the throbbing pain, I felt the comfort of my faith.

CHAPTER THIRTY-ONE
Valentine's Day

Valentine's Day is my favorite holiday. Not because I love getting valentines but because of what it stands for — showing the people you care about how much you love them. I so wish every day was Valentine's Day.

It had been six months of hell since Steve died — the misery of grief, a life of sadness — so not what our family was all about. As much as we felt our lives had been destroyed, I knew that God had a plan for us, and I was determined to figure out what he wanted us to do for him. It was time for new beginnings, and what better day to start over than one of my favorites, Valentine's Day. Enough of being sad and miserable, the girls and I needed to figure out some way to bless God for the life he had given us. I didn't know what that meant, but I was determined to figure it out.

Sara was away in South Africa, and I felt like she and God were figuring out her life. I knew that little valentine was taken care of. Amanda had dropped out of college in October and had moved back home. In January, she went back part-time and lived at home rather than on campus. Day by day, she too was learning to cope with our new life. She and I were struggling to figure out what to do with each other. Neither one of us had the strength to pretend anymore, yet getting real was messy and scary. I wasn't sure I had the strength for that either. Amanda needed help, and this time I didn't have what it took to help her. The best Valentine commitment I could make was to help her find the help she needed. Makena, our little five-year-old bundle of love, she too was finding her way without her daddy.

The girls were worried about how we were going to celebrate Valentine's Day without our valentine, Steve. They didn't want me to be sad and miss him, and they didn't know what to do to make it better. I needed to come up with a new tradition that would be a gift to my little women, rather than something else they did not have.

I told them that Valentine's Day was not about having a valentine; it was all about love — giving love, receiving love, expressing love, feeling love, anything to do with love. Since we loved each other so much, we could be each other's valentines, and since it was my favorite holiday, I thought we should celebrate it starting February first all the way through the fourteenth. For the first week, we would draw names and have a secret valentine. That way, we could feel the love every day. Then the next week, we would draw another name and do the same thing. We had so much love in our family that we needed fourteen days to celebrate instead of just one, and so the Secret Valentine's Day Love tradition began.

Those fourteen days were filled with silly gifts, simple smiles, and the wonderful sound of laughter as we unwrapped lots of love, day by day. I also wanted to bless our new home and fill it with memories of love, not death. What better day than Valentine's Day to throw a Thank You party for the friends that had been beside me on the journey of figuring out how to do life without Steve.

It was then, as I gently opened my heart back up to living, that I could feel the depth of knowing that we don't have forever. My heart ached for forever. I wanted the people that I loved to get a glimpse of the power of this knowing, that forever can end without notice. What did they want to do with their forever? Who did they want to spend it with? How could I help? I wanted to give them the gift of forever, starting on this Valentine's Day. I think that each one of us had learned something from watching death come in and steal our life's dreams away. We needed to claim our love for each other and get real about what mattered most — the people we were spending our forever with.

I had not even touched Steve's kitchen. I avoided it. Things had to change. So I decided I would get out all of his cookbooks, shop for all the familiar ingredients, and then together, with friends, we could make our favorite Steve dish. That was the party plan.

As I sat down to think about whom I wanted to invite, the list was short but filled with people that had changed my life. As I wrote each person's name, memories of how God had placed them in my life, at just the right time to connect my life to what he wanted next for me, became so obvious. The names seemed to find their way from my heart to my head. It was fascinating to put together a list of people that showed up so unexpectedly in my life, and then to realize how permanently their chapter had been written in my life story. Many of our friends did not know each other, but this Valentine's Day they would meet and share how Steve had touched their lives.

And so, Valentine's Day came, and so did our party. It felt like life had color again — not bold, vibrant colors but simple, splashes of color that made my black and white world begin to feel soft again. For the first time, our home was filled with those decadent smells of homemade food, fabulous wine, and the buzz of friends sharing love stories. What a blessing, what a gift of love. Thank you, God, for the beautiful colors our handpicked friends bring to our lives. I saw your love for me through their gentle eyes as they watched me hang on to my past yet inch my way into a future without Steve. Isn't that what Valentine's Day is all about? Celebrating love no matter what shade of color it shows up?

And to you, my dear Steve, I raise my glass. For all the love you have given me. For the people and projects that touched your soul. For the moments in time that now define our life together. For you and me. . .I wish forever would not have been so short.

With all my love,
C

CHAPTER THIRTY-TWO
Death, You Are So Cruel

Life was changing, but was I? My little women were finding their own way through grief, and our friends had said their good-byes at our Valentine's Day party. And now, my world was safe enough for me to spend some time alone, figuring out how I felt about it all. I did want to change. I did want to find out who I was without Steve, but what did that even mean? How could I live again without facing the death that had ripped my life apart? I wrote this letter, addressing it directly to death itself. . .

June 30, 2004, 4:15 p.m.
The day you came to visit.
July 28, 2004, 11:15 a.m.
The day you came to stay.
Today, March 8, 2005.
The day I wish you would pack your bags and go away!
  It is quite cruel the things you do. The way you come into our lives and steal away our hopes and dreams.
  I feel as though I have been frozen in time. I watch my life. I live my life. I do the things that are expected of me. Yet when I have an extra moment, I go back to the "me" that you have frozen. I begin to chisel away the layers of ice that have become my looking glass.
  I see you. I watch the dreadful things you do.
  I cannot get the visions of Steve's death to leave my view.
  I hear you.
  The sounds of Steve dying are deafening to me.
  I hear his breathing. I hear his struggle.
  I hear the silence. I hear our children scream. I hear our family sob.
  Why do you do this?
  Why are you so cruel?
  Is that your plan? Is that why you have chosen to freeze me in ice?
  Because it is clear. If you touch it, it is cold, it is stiff, and it is easily broken. The ice is transparent; to others, I appear to be the same.

Oh, dear Death, I do not wish to play your game.
My heart is still pounding, and it is the heat of my passion that will turn this block of ice into living water.
I will not miss another day.
Good-bye, Death. You may not stay!

CHAPTER THIRTY-THREE
Day By Day

It's amazing what a difference a year makes. This time last year, Steve and I were about to begin our final chapter of life together. We had no idea. We had made plans for this day — the day our remodel would be nearing completion — but not for the days that brought Steve's life to completion. If only we knew...would we have been different?

> Hi Babe,
>
> They started painting the outside of the house today. They taped up all the windows. They sealed up all the doors. Makena and I were inside. One minute we could see perfectly out the windows. We could come and go as we pleased. Our view of the world appeared to be clear. And then, some strangers came and placed a plastic film over our windows and our doors, and our view changed. I know that it is just a temporary thing. I know that all I have to do is take the plastic off of the windows and I will be able to see everything just as I always have. But from the inside looking out, it does not feel like that. I feel as though my life has been sealed off. That I know there is a beautiful world out there, but I can't see it anymore. I have lost my vision. I feel blinded by the pain. I wish it were as simple as taking the plastic off of my life to gain my view again.
>
> Makena said, "Mommy, how will we know when to wake up tomorrow if we can't see the sun?" I too wonder, am I going to wake up tomorrow...
>
> Tomorrow will come, that I know. The painters will return. The sun will shine. In a few days, the house will be painted. The plastic taken off of the windows. The walls will be painted a beautiful color, and our home will be closer to being finished. Is this true of my pain? Am I getting any closer to finishing this dreadful time? Oh dear God, I pray I am. I know I am such a wimp. It has not even been a year, yet I feel like I can't take another day of this lonely, sad, constant ache.
>
> Makena and I just finished our usual routine. We took a bubble bath, read our books, and she is snuggled up in our bed going to sleep with the

sound of the keyboard typing away to you. Dear God, this is so awful. I so miss you making my life so much more exciting than I do!

I guess I need to figure out who Carlette is. Who am I going to be without you? I think about what you would be doing if I had died. You would have carried on, continued working, continued reading each night, probably enjoying a glass of wine. You would cook Makena dinner, read to her, and then tuck her in. Would you miss me as much as I miss you? Would you feel as lost as I do? I know you would not have the pleasure of attending many events in my honor. For I have not lived a life worthy of honor. It makes me wonder why I am still here and you are home. You, my dear, were changing the world. I, my dear, was just oblivious to the fact that it was you who made everything work. You were just gracious enough to let me think I had anything to do with it.

I looked up a beach house in Carmel for the summer. I got sick to my stomach as I read the captions. I don't belong there. I don't have the foggiest idea where I belong. We have a beautiful home here. I just need to settle down here and figure out who and what God intended for my life. Enjoy eternity, my dear, for I will join you someday. I miss you. I love you. I don't know how in the world I am going to face another day, but I know I will . . .

With all my love,
C

CHAPTER THIRTY-FOUR
One Year Without Forever

I loved my quiet time in the mornings. The house was not yet filled with contractors, Makena was still enjoying her dreams, and reality had not yet woken up. This was when it felt safe for me to connect to my heart; it was okay to wonder how I was going to make it through the day. I was alone, so I could cry. No one had to know that on this particular morning, I did not want another day. . .And then as I sat, weak from trying to make it all work, I got an e-mail that reminded me that of course I could make it through another day. My little woman, Sara, halfway around the world, wanted to connect. . .

Thu 7/28/2005 4:13 AM
Hi Mom,

Happy Daddy Day. I just wanted to tell you I love you and I have been praying for the family today. I wanted to tell you how awesome God is. Today I did not really know how to get my head straight to have class discussions and all. I had the first period and I did not want to do it, but I got there and it was an English class. I had to teach two classes, so it was like 50 kids. I started with my life and then I got to Steve and told them today was one year. It was hard. I did not know if I could keep speaking because I was thinking about what I was doing at the time of day last year. But I did, and the class was so responsive. Two-thirds of the class gave their heart to the Lord. Afterwards the teacher wanted to talk to me. She has been serving God for six years and today she just wanted to take her class in the sun because it was cold. She heard my testimony, and it changed her life. She brought me a book to read. She had never read it, but she said, "I think God wants me to give it to you." It's called <u>Where Contentment and Desire Meet</u> by Kingsly Fletcher. God is watching over me, blessing me for sharing God's love even when it is so hard.

Last night we went to a play all about a girl whose dad died of cancer and how she felt so alone and was mad at God. In the end, she had to surrender to the Lord. It was really hard to watch, but God was preparing me for today. I could not block it out and not deal with it. God is carrying me through today and you too. I tell the world how you hold tight to God — don't let go. I love you so much and I am sorry I am not there today. I am in the right place though. I know it. I hope Monterey is nice and the family is good. Today is harder than I thought it would be probably because I am living it and feeling it. This is hard but necessary. I love you.

Say hello to Amanda and Kena. I will be praying for you all day. Be strong and give all the sadness to God. Today is a healing day for the Patterson family. I love you lots. Miss you. God is wrapping us in his arms today.

Love,
Sara

Sara had sent us her Daddy Day love note, and now it was time for Amanda, Makena, and me to live through the day that created Daddy Day. I needed to feel Steve's strength in my life today, as all of his little women faced the anniversary of our forever ending...

July 27, 2005
Hi Babe,

Well here we are — Amanda, Makena, and me in Monterey to be with you. We left Phoenix on Monday; flew to San Francisco; saw the sights and enjoyed the city. Tuesday, drove to Santa Cruz. We went on the train ride through the Redwoods. I shared with the girls your passion for such grand, strong, incredible trees. How you loved to stand next to them so that you didn't feel so tall. As I told the story, I realized how much you reminded me of Redwoods — tall, strong, grand in stature. And then we talked all about it. It came to me about how present God is in nature, and there he was — strong, grand, and bigger than life.

We then went to the beach and boardwalk. Makena ran right for the water, finally free to feel the waves! It was beautiful. She laughed. She wiped out. She cried. She came to me for comfort. We laughed. We said good-bye to the beach and dusted off our sandy feet until another day.

The rides were okay. Nothing I am too crazy about. Makena loved the roller coasters. As I sat there riding it over and over, I thought of you a year ago...riding the roller coaster of life. Today, last year, was your final ride. I remember every moment of it. Just as I feel right now — a bit sick, ready for the ride to end, and not really up for anything else — just ready to go home...and the ride ends.

We drove to Monterey. It felt so much like home, I was amazed. Makena got sick to her tummy, too much junk and fun at the park. We checked into the hotel. I tucked the girls in and went right over to see your grave.

Oh it felt so good to be back with you! Strange, I know, yet not strange to my heart and soul! And so, as I sat with you at your grave, I opened my Bible, and this is what you gave me ... "All kinds of trials...have come so that your faith — of greater worth than gold, which perishes even though refined by fire — may be proved genuine." 1 Peter 1:6-7.

I love you,
C

July 28, 2005

Your last day here on earth, a year ago. Oh how I wish I knew so many things. I thought of you all day yesterday and last night, wondering what you were feeling on these days. I woke up feeling awful today, just so aware of what happened to us — how our lives changed forever today!

I am amazed at how deep the pain penetrates my soul and the souls of our children. What do we do with all of this pain? How can we begin to heal from such a huge wound that feels raw and aches every minute of the day and night?

I feel so sad today, so lonely, and so empty. I feel so empty because I have spent the last year trying to do everything right for you and I am empty. I have nothing left to give. I have wanted to make sure all the children's hearts and souls were sheltered from this dreadful pain. And although I know that to be an impossible task, I felt I had to try.

Sometimes the pain is so deep I wonder how I am going to draw my next breath. Other times when I brace myself for the pain, it seems okay and I feel as though we have made peace. Like yesterday...

I took Amanda and Makena to your grave. It was the first time they had been there since last year. I was dreading this moment. It was such a terrible, cold moment for me when I first saw your grave, and I did not want their precious hearts to have to feel such pain. Well, they reacted so differently. Makena wanted her picture taken by your headstone. She wanted to take pictures of Amanda and me with you. There was calm about our time at your grave. It was as if the girls felt like we were all together again. It was an amazing feeling. We spent the next hour walking around reading all the other headstones. We even found another Patterson.

We will spend the day at the Spirit West Coast Christian Music Festival, so kind of you to arrange this for us! It would be an awful day just reliving all the memories of last year. I am so grateful that we get to go and praise God, sing and worship him — a perfect way to embrace your first anniversary in heaven.

Oh how I love you and thank you for all that you have done for our family. Thank you so much for loving us and preparing our new home for us in heaven. I look forward to moving in with you some day!

I just opened my Bible as I finished writing to you. I opened it to Numbers 28, wow, what a strong message. I am always so amazed at how you and God communicate so perfectly and so strong! Thank you!

July 29, 2005
Hi Babe,

Well, you have been gone now 25 hours and 1 year. You have been a wonderful husband, an incredible gift, a friend I feel so blessed to have spent years with, a father to our children, the list goes on and on. The amazing thing about you dying is that is has woken me up. I don't even have to put the words together anymore — you know my heart, you hear my questions just as I am figuring them out. It is sweet how you don't answer until I ask. I have complete faith in you. You had to die for this to happen — wow — I wonder why.

I thank you for the gift of life. For showing me how to celebrate each day. For giving me love in so many ways.

With all my love,
C

CHAPTER THIRTY-FIVE
Love Blesses

Many years ago when Steve and I fell in love, we shared our hopes and dreams for what we hoped our lives were going to be like. We both loved our children and felt they were absolutely the best part of our story. Steve also shared a longing that he had given up on — he had always wanted a little girl in addition to his great boys. I felt blessed to have Amanda and Sara become the little girls that he never had. We settled into life as a blended family, and the simple times of sitting around talking about our hopes and dreams were replaced with just keeping up with life.

It was October of 1998 and we were both craving a weekend in the wine country, so we packed up for a few days of nothing but wine and love. It was wonderful, just the two of us spending time reconnecting and beginning to dream again.

We returned home, and I was not feeling too well in the weeks that followed. I had my yearly gynecologist appointment already scheduled months in advance. Much to my surprise, when I was at my appointment and shared with my doctor that I had not been feeling well, she knew why. I was pregnant. It had been fourteen years since I had heard those words.

Steve and I went to dinner that night, and as usual, he ordered us a glass of wine. But things were not going to be the usual anymore. I changed my order to a glass of water, and with a simple twinkle of the eye, we both knew life was going to get very interesting.

And now again, many years later, here I was taking care of his little woman. He was gone, but he kept showing up in all the new and old things we were doing. . .

Hi Babe,

Well, here we are again, another month gone by without you. We are doing okay.

I just bought a ticket to South Africa. So you, so not me! I know this trip will be amazing. I know it is part of God's amazing plan for Sara and me. I can feel his hand in our journey. I am learning to enjoy the unknown rather than to fear it. I guess you have taught me this in your abrupt change of plans.

The girls and I were watching home videos last night. Watching Makena's birth and all the memories as she learned to walk and talk and begin to become Makena. We all supported her every move. We cheered her on just for being her. I love the way you looked at her, with such love and acceptance. She did not need to do a thing to have your love, just showing up, and she was in! Wow, what a gift.

What a blessing she has been to us, and us to her. What were just fun moments recorded on video have now become one of our connections to you. We watch your every move. We listen to your voice, your laughter, your words. They are magic to us, and we try to reconnect with you and that moment. We laugh. We cry. We feel so empty. We feel so lonely. We feel so much. All because of you, my dear. You, just being you.

Funny how this family thing works. You and I fall in love. Our love connects Amanda and Sara to you. You change their lives. You give yourself to them. You teach them what you know. You share your hopes and dreams with them. You take them to favorite places of yours. You begin to share yourself with them by sharing your story. By sharing your favorites. And then our love creates Makena, and the cycle starts all over again. So simple.

It is so strange how we think this is going to go on forever. We think we will be taking those family trips to places that everyone moans and groans about — forever. And then in a moment's time, it's over. The end of your story as you will tell it. Your time is up. Without warning, we come to your last chapter. Wow, I am so shocked at the ending.

What is amazing to me is how your story continues without you. I now tell the girls about things that we laughed about, things that we loved, and things that seemed so silly. And then I notice them telling your story. Sharing something that you said or did with someone they know. All this happening with you gone for 14 months.

I marvel at how the chapters of this story continue to be written. I am amazed at life. I am amazed at your life. I am amazed at our lives now. Oh I could tell you the details of things we are doing, but I know you know what we are doing. I know you are protecting and guiding us in our everyday life. I thank you for loving us from so far away. I thank you for always being there when I call your name. I thank you for letting me try to make it on my own, and then when I can't take it another minute, you make it all work. I thank you for showing me love.

With all my love,
C

Separated by many continents, it was the written word that kept our family together. We were all living in different time zones — Sara in South Africa, Steve in Heaven, and me in Phoenix, but our hearts beat to our very own family love zone. Whether it was with pen and paper or a keyboard and Internet connection, we needed to share our thoughts and what was happening in our lives with one another. It seemed to matter — or at least it desperately mattered to us at the time. We needed to feel connected to each other.

Even though Sara was so far away, I did not want her to miss any "Makena Moments," so I shared them with her in hopes that when she wandered into an Internet café, wanting to know what was happening at home, she would be able to read about a few simple conversations that had taken place between me and Makena. The following are e-mails from me to Sara, sharing those Makena Moments.

Mon 9/5/2005 1:54 PM
Hi Champ,

Makena and I were chatting about life, our usual conversation, and she said, "Mom, I am really proud of you" I asked why, and she said because I was famous. I asked why she thought I was famous, and she said because I was in the phone book and that was so cool!

So I am here to tell you that if you are listed in the phone book, consider yourself famous! And all this time we thought we had to do something special to be famous. . .

Love you!

Fri 9/9/2005 8:24 PM

Tonight as I was tucking Makena in, she asked me if her guardian

angel was a teenager or an old person. She hopes it is a teenager because she likes teenagers better than old people.
xoxoxo

Sun 9/11/2005 11:36 AM
"Mom, is Elvis real or just a character on Lelo and Stitch?"
"He was real. He was a famous singer who is dead now."
"Was he a good singer?"
"Yes."
"Wow, just think, Dad gets to meet Elvis!"
Life is good — Steve and Elvis are together, rejoice!!!!

Day by day, each one of us was making peace with our new normal.

CHAPTER THIRTY-SIX
More Reality

Sara had been in South Africa for a little more than eight months. Steve had been gone for fourteen months. We were all facing the reality that the life we were living now was it — this was how things were going to be now. We were all tired. We had tried so hard to be strong for each other, but our spirits were low, and it was tough to find new ways to convince ourselves that we were going to be okay.

Not a day went by that I did not send Sara an e-mail. Many days would pass without word from her, but I chose not to let my mind wander into darkness and just always prayed for her to be safe and to feel how much she was loved even though she was so far from home. Finally, I heard back from her...

Sun 9/11/2005 1:47 AM
Hi Mom,

Thank you for all your emails. This past week was awful. I was very sick with a fever, the flu, and a sore throat. I have been sick for five days. Today I am not well, but it's the first day I feel better not worse. The past week was hard. We lived in the middle of nowhere in the wilderness with too many bugs and snakes. We were in Zulu country, African tribal place. We are now at the beach, so I am a lot better. We are going to live in a Children's Home this upcoming week, so that should be better.

I am so sad lately. I cry and cry. I am crying now, but there is no reason, I am just always sad. I feel so stupid. I just cry. I want to come home. I don't like this anymore. My feelings are just hurt. I am so sad, but I don't know why. I just want to leave. I don't care anymore. I am tired of being sick, hurt, and not fitting in. I want to be home with my friends being myself...I am just not happy. Please keep praying for me. I need it so much.

My hair is really pretty — that is good in my life, and I am at the beach today, so that is good too. Please pray that I stop crying. I can't help it — it's not fun. I love you and keep emailing me and I will check it as soon as I can. I have one minute left so I love you lots xoxoxoxoxoxoxo.
Sara

I woke up and found that at 1:47 a.m., my little woman, Sara, had been sitting at an Internet café somewhere on the beach. As I was sleeping, she was crying. I had missed connecting with her, but I knew that sometime on another day she would sit down at a computer and be able to read what I had to say...

> Sun 9/11/2005 8:06 AM
> Hi My Fabulous Little Woman,
> I am so sorry you are hurting in so many ways — it breaks my heart! I am glad that you are crying, that is your grief being released. You must cry to heal, so just know that you are healing.
> Do you really want to come home? You know if you do I will have you home in a heartbeat. Please pray about it and let me know. I will continue to pray and have everyone I know pray for you. It is completely fine for me for you to come home. I know you have done incredible work and I am so proud of you! I know that you doing this has opened your heart and connected you to yourself and God. I am sure that is why you are so sad and crying so much. You have spent years denying yourself YOU and that is very sad and your heart and soul have so much to grieve about. But I know you are healing, and for that I thank God and you for having the courage to open up and begin the healing process.
> Pray for God to tell us what to do. He knows what is best. You know that as your mom I will have you on the next flight home. If you feel that is what God wants for you.
> Sending tons of love, blessings, tlc, hugs, love, and more love!

When times got tough for Sara, she reached for something or someone to make her feel better. I knew she was not doing well. I knew her heart and soul were facing the loneliness that she had felt her whole life. But I needed her to figure out how to find her way back to who she wanted to be, not the person that gave in to drugs or alcohol to make the pain go away — that was her past. I prayed for her to find her future in God's love and in the life that he had planned for her. Would it be too tough for her to do this? Only she and God would be able to figure this out, but not a day or night went by that that was not my prayer.

Sara and I talked on the phone and decided that she would do her very best to stay in South Africa and complete her program. Could she do it? Could I let her stay and go through the pain? Neither one of us was sure we had anything left to even try to finish out the program. If Sara did want to come home, however, I wanted her to do it the right way, not do something wrong to get sent home—that was her old way of handling things.

As I prayed without ceasing, I received this e-mail from her counselor...

Monday, September 12, 2005 1:45 PM
Dear Carlette,

I received your email this morning and felt the urgency to reply as soon as possible. I have spoken to Arrie, Sandra Jordaan and Eljoh (Sara's team leader) and feel I want to share the following with you:

Sara has a very special place in my heart. Since she came, I knew that she's a brave lady that is fighting the battle of life to come out a winner at the end. She is also part of fallen man, like any one of us, and sometimes tries and copes with her circumstances by not running to God. But God's grace has taken her from the valley to the mountains and He deserves all the glory for this.

I personally spoke to Eljoh this afternoon and specifically asked her about Sara's health. She confirmed that Sara had the flu last week, but that she received medicine and is recovering. She is still coughing at present which indicates the aftermath of the flu. It seems like she hurt her ankle during basketball coaching, but it was also reported to me how well Sara did with the kids and that she totally loved it − you can imagine!

Carlette, I think the real factor here is that she is feeling like being in a valley again; that she is feeling alone. Please allow me to share with you the situation.

The last conversation I had with her was on the phone...It was not one that I liked to have with her, but I felt it necessary at the time. It was about a smoking incident during their outreach time which she admitted to. I told her that this was her last warning and that if there was trouble in this area again, we would have to get her down to Stellenbosch for a week of evaluation. She agreed that she understood this. After this, she became good friends with a guy on the team, but unfortunately, he wasn't the best influence on her at that stage. From our point of view, this friendship meant that the team split into two groups − Sara and him forming the one. The guy has some struggles and we had to take him off the team for the sake of the functionality of the rest of the team. Sara didn't feel the problem lied with him and I assume immediately felt like an outsider in her team loosing this friend.

I have challenged Eljoh today as leader to really focus on serving Sara so that she could feel accepted. I also reminded her of the importance of this Christian experience to be a good one for Sara's life for the sake of her future. Eljoh agreed to continue doing this.

We feel that if they could spent some time with her on a one to one basis and look into the team situation, this could be perfect timing from God. I know though that no one's skills can change someone's attitude. This applies to each member of the School's Team.

Sandra Jordaan and Adri (my girlfriend) also would love to encourage her over the phone. They both love her dearly and would hate seeing her leave to go home without giving it a very brave and good run. We, here at SCAS HQ, would also love to see her complete this year. I appreciate that it must be really hard for you and no one can make the decisions for you. I just felt to share some background to my observation of this situation.

Let's pray for determination, perseverance, peace and joy. I pray that this year at SCAS will be something good to reflect on in Sara's life when she looks back.

Please continue this conversation with me – I will make the time to communicate as much as possible with you on this matter.

Could Sara make a different choice and begin a different life, or was her past just too strong for her? Oh, dear God, I do pray for your strength to take over and for Sara to feel your love over her hatred for herself and her life. Through God all things are possible, and this was the message I needed Sara to hear from me, over and over and over. . .

Tue 9/20/2005 5:03 AM
Hi Mom,

I just read all the emails. Thanks for all the support and that everyone is willing to help me. This week is good — we are out a lot learning about the Hindu religion, so that is very interesting. I am living on a cow farm, which is not that bad. We are out all day. The people are very nice and it's a good home. We get to go to Durban on Saturday. It's a huge city with a big mall and an ocean. So that's cool. I am still coughing, so I made a doctor appointment on Thursday. Hope it goes well. I should get some medicine or something. I bought Vitamin C with the credit card yesterday and I am taking it, so I hope it helps.

I am working very hard on my attitude and loving the team, but every time I get ahead, something happens, but I am not stopping trying. Keep up the prayers please.

I am going to a man to get prayed for in two days. That should be awesome. He is like the lady I liked so much who did counseling and deliverance. So I will let you know how that goes. He is the man who has been teaching us all week, so it is part of our lecture today to each get prayed for.

I might even be going horseback riding, I don't know yet. I'm not a fan of animals, but I am trying to have fun with the team. We'll see.

I love you very much and thank you for helping me and listing to all my sorrows about the team and my life. I do feel better now, not so much anger inside. I gave my testimony today at a school and counseled some girls, so God is still working through me. My heart has more peace, and I feel okay. There is only forty days till we go back to the Island. I can do it. Forty days is not so long. Just pray for peace and love to flow out of me. I love you lots and lots, but I have to go now. I love you.

Sara

Though one was on a farm in South Africa, and the other one was in a beautiful pink princess bedroom in Phoenix, Sara and Makena were both trying to figure out how to manage their grief. Two sisters, many years apart and separated by many continents, feeling like maybe it was too much. I wanted Sara to know that she was not alone in her up-and-down journey of navigating through grief . . .

Fri 9/23/2005 8:57 AM
Hi Champ,

I wanted to share this with you, I thought you would know the feeling. . . Makena woke up today crying and said, "I am just having a tender heart day. Can I stay home from school?" I said, "Of course, I love you, just go curl up and relax." A bit later, I asked how she was feeling. She said, "Mom, my heart just says, I just can't take it anymore!"

xoxoxoxoxo

Sara had survived her forty days and was back on the main island for the final days of her program. Now at the end of October, she was going to turn twenty-one and be able to celebrate having completed an amazing year of transformation. One way for both of us to hold on and make it to graduation was for her to know that I would come to South Africa and be there to watch her graduate.

Mon 10/24/2005 8:26 PM
Hi Champ!

I am so excited to see you. I can't believe you are in South Africa. It did not seem so crazy of an idea for you to be there until I had to start thinking about going there. . .I am in shock! This is so out of my comfort zone. Never in my wildest dreams would I have ever imagined me going to South Africa, much less to celebrate my little woman graduating from a Year of Service! Wow! I am so proud of you! I am proud of you for getting well and being able to stay. I hope it has been a good experience for you!

I will be there on Monday, November 7th and then fly out on the same day as you do.

What are you going to do for your birthday? Any wild and crazy plans? I hope so! The big 21 wow! Are you one of the oldest kids in the program? Is 21 a special birthday in South Africa? Just think, for Amanda's 21, we were at Post Ranch Inn, and for yours, South Africa, I am in shock. . .can you tell?

Just think, a year ago you were in rehab right now. . .so many things have changed. Like I keep saying. . .I am so proud of what you have done with your year!

Okay, my fabulous little woman. . .that's all for me. Any news from your side of the world?

I hope I get to hear from you before your birthday, but if not. . .

HAPPY BIRTHDAY TO YOU.
HAPPY BIRTHDAY TO YOU
HAPPY BIRTHDAY, DEAR MY FABULOUS LITTLE WOMAN,
HAPPY BIRTHDAY TO YOU!!!!

I LOVE YOU!!!

Little did Sara know that I was coming to South Africa early to surprise her for her birthday. Bags packed with glow sticks, party favors, candy, and as much American stuff as I could find, I boarded a plane to go halfway around the world to celebrate making it through twenty-one years of life with my little woman, Sara.

All the SCAS kids were returning from their different missions on that day. It would be the first time they had been back together in quite some time. I arrived at the SCAS campus before they did and hid out until Sara arrived. As soon as she got out of the van, they blindfolded her and brought her to where I was waiting for her, but she still didn't know I was there. All of her friends made a circle around her and started singing "Happy Birthday." As they started the second verse, I started singing with them. Sara was still blindfolded. As she heard my voice, she started screaming, and I started crying. She took off the blindfold, and we hugged and hugged. What a birthday celebration — what a gift of life for both of us. It had been quite the year, and we were both ready to celebrate.

We unpacked my huge suitcase of party stuff, turned on the music, turned off the lights, passed out the glow sticks, and danced all night! Happy Birthday, Sara.

Thank you, God, for all your blessings of love and grace!

CHAPTER THIRTY-SEVEN
Makena's Love Notes to Her Daddy

Makena wanted a way to tell her daddy how she was feeling. As much as we talked about him and shared stories about him, she wanted and needed more. Since writing to Steve had become the way Amanda, Sara, and I were coping, I thought maybe Makena would find peace by writing to him too. I bought her a journal, and she too began to share her heart with Steve through the amazing healing power of paper and pen.

June 24, 2005 (Age 6)
Happy Birthday Daddy. I love you. When you died, I didn't want to leave the house with Gi Gi and Papa because I was afraid something bad was going to happen to you.

Makena had a present for her daddy on his birthday. She went in her room and brought out a handful of marbles. She put them in a small box, wrapped the box, and set it by the journal. She said she gave her daddy the marbles because she remembered him teaching her how to play.

Another Day, 2005
I miss you Daddy. Do you miss me?
What is it like in Heaven?

October 4, 2005
I miss you Daddy
Why did you have to leave?
Please don't forget me in Heaven.

Another Day, 2005
Dear Daddy,
Today I was thinking about the time I went to work with you. . .do you remember everything we did together on earth or have you forgotten now that you are in Heaven?
Do you remember sliding down the hill that was covered with snow, on

*your bummy when you were here on earth? I do, we had so much fun.
I will never forget everything that we did.
I miss you, I wish you were here.
Today at school we talked about the Dad's Barbeque, remember when we went last year. I am so sad that you won't be able to go with me anymore. Lauren said I could pretend that her dad is my dad too, but I don't want to, I just want you. Mom said I did not have to go, but I want to go, just wish you were here. I am sure Mom will figure something out for me. I am sorry for all the bad things I did today, I didn't mean to do them.
I Love You*

Writing to Steve was our new normal. Anytime something special happened, instead of picking up the phone to share it with the person I loved, I picked up a pen and blank piece of paper and found a quiet moment to tell Steve all about it. . .

*Another Day, 2005
Hi Babe,
    Makena lost her first tooth today. . .very exciting. When I tucked her in, we wrote a note to the tooth fairy letting her know that she wanted to keep the tooth but please leave money. When we said her prayers that night, she told you all about it. She said, "Someday when I see you again, Daddy, I am going to have all grown-up teeth, but other than that, I will look the same. I just wanted you to know that I love you all day and all night even though you are not here with me. . .I will never forget you!"*

Makena was growing up. She looked like any other little girl. She went to school, she hoped for play dates, she cried when a friend hurt her feelings, she loved ice cream, she appeared to be normal. But her heart hurt, and she knew this was not normal. She wanted to make the hurt stop, but something about the hurt also connected her to her daddy and she did not want to stop thinking about him. She was a thinker just like her daddy. I could tell when she entered the "thinking world" she did not seem like a little girl anymore. She seemed to go somewhere, mentally, that helped her sort her feelings. She got to be mad or sad or confused, and methodically, she took each puzzle piece of grief and studied it. She wanted to know what to do with it and how it was going to fit into her life picture.

Makena's pure thinking and open heart believed whatever I told her. If I said that her daddy loved her and was with her every minute of the day, she believed me. If she had a question that I knew Steve would know the answer to, I would tell her to ask her daddy. In her beautiful, childlike voice, she would ask him. And for a few moments, I could tell the two of them were communicating. She would smile. Her eyes would twinkle. And then, very matter of fact, she would tell me what her daddy said. It was amazing. She didn't need it to make sense to others because she trusted me to make sense of her new world.

Once again, only by picking up a pencil, or crayon, and sitting quietly with a blank piece of paper, did the words and emotions seem to find some place to go. Makena knew she needed time with her daddy, and this became the way she grew up with him living in heaven. . .

April 8, 2006
How is Heaven?
I had a sleepover with Katie. Now I know how to do the Macarena dance.
Are you proud of me? I hope so.
I love u Dad

April 28, 2006
Hi Dad,
I'm sick. You are lucky you can't get sick in Heaven.
I got sick on Daddy Day.
I want to see you one more time.
Please remember I love you and Grandpa.

October 22, 2006
Hi Dad,
I am 7 years old.
I am in the second grade.
I still miss you a lot.

December 24, 2006
It is Christmas Eve Daddy. I would give anything for you to be here.
I love you.

Another Day, 2007
I need you now Daddy.
I miss you lots and lots.
I wish you would come back Daddy.
My world is not the same without you.

March 12, 2007
I'm so glad Sara gave me her Little Pet Shop.
My favorite is Rusty. He is a brown little dog.
Things are going good around here.
But it would be better with you.
I love you

May 30, 2007
I can't believe that I'm out of the second grade! Even though I've gotten sad you always made me happy. I hope your life in Heaven is great.
I can't wait to see you again.

November 13, 2007 (Age 8)
Dear Daddy,
I can't believe Grace is in the hospital. She is one of my best friends.
Now I only have Katie. The rest of the girls are mean.

When I read <u>Where is Waldo</u> I think of you because we always read that book together.
I love you and miss you so much.
Life is not the same without you.
I don't have anyone to hug. Anyone besides Mom that is.
I love you!

Another Day, 2008 (Age 9)
I loved being in your arms when you sang our special song to me.
I wish you could still sing to me.
Hearing your voice is like hearing the angels sing.
You were the best person that I could go to when I was sad.
I loved it when you took our family on every trip possible.
I loved how much you loved basketball.
You are why the sun comes up every day and sets on the mountains.
You are why the ocean has waves.
I love you with <u>all</u> my heart.

Another Day, 2008
I remember all the times you and I went swimming.
When I think about you my heart is filled with joy.
Even though you aren't with me I think of you every minute of every day.
I remember when you took our family to Hume Lake.
I had a lot of fun.
I know how much you love me.
Being with you was like floating on a cloud.
You are the best Dad I could ever dream of.
With <u>a lot</u> of love.

When Makena was nine years old, she wrote this poem about her life. It was published in Inspired 2009 Poetry Collection:

> "About Me"
> On June 18 I entered the world
> A bundle of joy a cute little girl.
> My name is Makena after the beach
> Where my parents got married and thought of me.
> My daddy was with me for 5 golden years
> Then tragedy happened and he disappeared.
> When he died my eyes filled with tears
> Because I lost a beautiful soul who loved me so dear.
> My heart soon mended and then I grew tall
> To a wonderful girl who went through it all.
> And now I'm in 4th grade with an amazing teacher
> Whose heart is pure gold and cares for us all through sadness and joy and all in-between.
> This teacher is Raimie she's like a queen.
> My goals in life are to play volleyball
> With a swing in my step and not ever fall.
> My life is like no other
> I am an individual
> There's no one like me
> And I'm like no other.
> The moral to the story is I'm me.

CHAPTER THIRTY-EIGHT
Finding Hope

It had been two years since Steve died, and I found that the layers of grief were creating new layers of life. It was as though I could recognize a painful moment — appearing in black and white — and then as I stayed with it, colors filled the picture and it resembled my memory of Steve, yet it was different.

I liked the new tapestry that was being woven with my sadness. The threads of my life with Steve were giving strength and color to the new vision that I could not yet see. I gave thanks to the grief for holding me in a safe place as I found my way from death to new life.

I woke up one morning with a feeling of complete contentment. That feeling and I were able to connect just moments before my logical brain was awake. As I opened my eyes to wonder why I was feeling so good, I noticed that nothing in my life had changed; no one was in bed with me, and life appeared to be just as I left it when I went to sleep.

Ah, but I felt like I was awakening from a night of bliss — a night spent with my lover, understanding every word we shared, entangled bodies touching as one. Yet I had spent the night alone — sad, crying, being present with my memories of lost love. And then I understood that Steve was with me during that pain. It was him I spent the night with. It was letting go of our pain that made me wake up to such bliss.

I wanted more of that brief taste of bliss that had just touched my life.

Life didn't make sense the way it used to. Things that used to bring me comfort were now bringing me pain. I felt suffocated in memories. The more of Steve's things I held on to, the lonelier I became. And so piece by piece, I began to let go of Steve's stuff, even though I was afraid that if I let go of his stuff I would be letting go of him. Much to my surprise, the more of his stuff I let go of, the more room I had in my life and in my heart to feel his love.

When I want to go back in time, I now go to that sacred place where I keep my memories of Steve. The memories are so vivid. I can hear our conversations. I can feel his touch. I can smell the aromas. Not a detail is lost. At the time, I didn't know that day would become a memory vaulted in my bank of consciousness or that it would become my lifeline to us. Now knowing that, I understand how precious our moments are, how they become our life when they're woven together.

CHAPTER THIRTY-NINE
Amanda's Turn

Amanda graduated from college with an associate's degree. I was so proud of her for not giving up. She spent five years at college, lived in the dorm for some of it, and worked part-time for most of it. All of this from a daughter the doctors said to give up on — to give up on my "normal" hopes and dreams for Amanda because she was not going to be able to live a "normal" life. Who gets to define "normal"? Thank you, God, for your amazing grace and for Amanda!

It was time for another celebration — our family's first college graduation. I was so proud of Amanda!

By this time, we had been able to diagnose Amanda with Asperger's Syndrome and had found some help for her and for me on how best to support her. She was not a kid anymore, and we were both going to have to figure out what her future looked like.

Steve and I had agreed that if it was financially possible, we would pay for the children to get their college degrees and then they would be on their own. We hadn't talked about what being on their own looked like, and now here it was, that time, and I wasn't sure what to do next.

Amanda was able to get full-time jobs, but she wasn't able to keep them. For the next couple of years, Amanda and I struggled to figure out our relationship. Our home wasn't peaceful. Amanda and I were constantly arguing about boundaries and expectations. She felt entitled to live in my home but wanted to act however she pleased. In her mind, my rules didn't apply to her anymore. She wanted independence, yet she relied on me for everything. That wasn't good for either of us. I was wearing down. The load of being a single mom, going back to work full-time, supporting Sara in college, and raising a young daughter was catching up with me. I was too tired to keep struggling with Amanda.

I told Amanda she needed to come up with a plan to move out and begin working toward living on her own. I didn't set a time limit, but I wanted to begin thinking about it and exploring what this looked like for both of us. I wasn't sure what to do, but I knew that what I had been doing wasn't working and I needed relief soon.

Unfortunately, once again, God and I weren't on the same page. I was making plans without him. It seemed like I had used up my quota of "Dear God, help," and I felt like it was up to me to come up with what to do with Amanda. Yeah right. You can imagine how well that went over!

The next year went something like this. . .

Amanda decided she was going to move to a homeless shelter. I supported her idea. I told her to leave her credit card and her keys to our home behind. She could take her phone because I wanted us to be able to stay in contact. She packed her suitcase, taking some Pop-Tarts, her journals, a few changes of clothes, some water — you know, the basic essentials you need at a homeless shelter. She left, boarded the bus, headed to the homeless shelter. I had no idea what was going to happen next and was too exhausted to think about it.

An hour later, I got a call from Amanda. She had decided she didn't want to move into the homeless shelter. I asked her what she wanted me to do for her. She wanted to come home. I said she could, but only if she followed my rules. She came home, unpacked her suitcase, put the Pop-Tarts back in the cabinet, and we sat down for a heart to heart.

And so the counseling for both of us began.

It was time to unpack all of Amanda's hurts and disappointments. Time to get real and face the fact that life had been tough on her and my way of pushing through it was not working anymore. We had to find a new way, and both of us were broken enough to know we couldn't do it alone. Thank goodness God took my call. He told me he had been waiting to hear from me, and he welcomed Amanda and me into his loving embrace. He had a plan for both of us, but I had been too stubborn to consider it. For his plan to work, I had to admit that Amanda was different, and that different was exactly how God needed her to be for the work he created her to do. I had to let go and let God take it from there.

Day by day, Amanda and I wrestled with the truth of what it meant to have Asperger's — for both of us. We got help and began our journey of healing. The help that God blessed us with was an organization called Southwest Autism Research & Resource Center (SARRC). The organization was made up of angels that surrounded our family as we struggled through the endless maze of what it meant to accept autism into our life. Our family is healthy and happy today because of that organization and its amazing staff.

With SARRC now a trusted family member, for the first time, Amanda and I were facing our truth. It was my prayer that through God's love and grace, we would be set free of our sadness about what we both wished life had been.

Every day, as Amanda struggled to find her way and I struggled to let her, I held on to the scripture, "Then you will know the truth, and the truth will set you free." John 8:32.

My Grandmother Lewis was a Christian Science reader. Every Sunday, as I sat in church as a little girl, I would draw a picture of what I saw as I listened to her read the lesson. Behind her were two large blue signs, one with the scripture "Then you will know the truth, and the truth will set you free." John 8:32. I don't remember what was on the other sign, but the image of my grandmother reading, with that scripture in the background, served as a lifeline when Amanda and I were finding our way back to each other.

My mom's dad was a Primitive Baptist preacher. So every other Sunday we would attend his church. It was so different from the Christian Science service. We would sit in a small church on hard, wooden benches and sing hymns. We would take turns going to the front to lead the hymns. A few of my favorites were "Heavenly Sunlight," "Trust and Obey," and "Count Your Many Blessings." I haven't spent much time in the Baptist faith, but the words to those songs, imprinted on my heart and soul as a child, proved to be all I needed to understand how to do life with Amanda.

It's quite amazing that when I was young, God was writing the lyrics to my life song: know the truth, and the truth will set you free; heavenly sunlight, heavenly sunlight flooding my soul with glory divine; trust and obey, for there's no other way to be happy in Jesus but to trust and obey; count your blessings, name them one by one, count your blessing, see what God hath done! Amanda unlocked what God had placed in my heart as a child — the way he wanted me to live as an adult.

CHAPTER FORTY
Daddy Day Love Notes from Sara

Sara came home from South Africa a different little woman. She returned in November, and by January she was enrolled in college in California. We had spent a couple months transitioning back to life in the USA, went to counseling, and were slowly, but very intentionally, going to do life differently — whatever that meant. Sara was going to leave home again, but this time her heart and soul were healing. Some things would be different, but some things would be the same. She would keep her Daddy Day journal close and know that whenever she needed her dad, he was just a blank piece of paper and pen away. The following are some of Sara's journal entries from that time. . .

January 28, 2007
Dear Steve,

It has been exactly 2 years since I wrote to you. So much has changed in my life, but I'm sure you're watching from above. The family is finally on the better side of things, instead of the worst, including me. Mom is like my best friend. I like being around her, Makena, and Amanda. For once in my life, I love our family. There is still a void without you. I still miss you and I still cry a lot, but I don't hate you anymore! I love you and I just get sad.

I made straight A's for the first time in my whole life! I am a freshman at Concordia University and on the Dean's List! Who would have ever thought I could pull that off. I am a changed person. I am sorry you didn't get to see the better me. I owe everything to God! He never gave up on me and I am coming around.

Well, it is the start of a new year and good things are going to happen.
I love you,
Happy Daddy Day

March 28, 2007
Dear Steve,

Happy Daddy Day! Guess what? Today is your special day for this month and I am glad. Lately I have been really depressed, sad, and lonely. You know the basics, but today I actually had a good day. It was like out of nowhere the depression just got up and left. Praise the Lord!

So today isn't a sad day for me and I'm sure not for you up there in Paradise. Down here on earth, things are pretty much the same. Our family is doing better though. Things just seem to be falling into place and running smoothly. Mom and I are like best friends! I truly like being around her and I actually prefer to be around her than other friends. We are both at peace with each other and I genuinely love her! Our relationship with each other is amazing and something I would have never imagined possible. I love Makena as well and have been spending time with her and her friends. She is a lot like you — a deep thinker and a huge reader! She is a natural basketball coach, not a player. She knows all the girls and how to play the game but won't step foot on the court with those "sweaty girls." Pretty funny.

Amanda has lost so much weight! She is exercising and counting her calories, a huge change. She is now working on her inner self and finding a job. So she is working hard to figure out Amanda.

We are all pulling through things. We never forget you! I never forget about you! You have your own family holiday — Daddy Day! I love you and I am glad to have you as my father. Say hello to Jesus for me, please.

September 28, 2007
Dear Dad,

The months keep passing by, and every day you are gone longer than before. Time here on earth never stops, it just keeps on going. Now, I am back in college, sitting in my dorm room on your special day. It is hard to imagine that I would ever be here if you were still alive. Maybe I wouldn't have been here at all if you were still alive. I know when you lived on earth I screwed up way more than I did things right, but I think I am finally a daughter you can be proud of.

This is my second year at Concordia University and I am still going strong. Last year I got straight A's both semesters! That means I made the Dean's List! Who would have ever thought I could get all A's? And I have not drank, smoked, done drugs, or dated/kissed any boys in a little over a year! So many accomplishments in life. I know you can watch me down here on earth and I'm glad you can see the new me.

Mom is doing well in her life. Makena is so grown up and doing such an awesome job at life! She is so smart and innocent and full of love. I know if you could hug her you would never let her go. She is half of you, like a little jewel you left behind, a reminder of you.

I miss the family now, being here at school away from them. I am getting older — 23 next month. I don't want to grow older and have to be an adult. I just want to be with Mom and the family forever. The older I get, the closer it gets to my independence and I don't want it! Never in a million years would I think I'd feel this way, but I do. You dying changed everything. At first everything just got worse, but now it is just different. I am glad you are not suffering in pain here on earth anymore, but I don't like that all the photos of you seem outdated. It feels like so long since you have been around, like a whole other life has happened.

I love you and I know you had to die. I miss you even though I know you are in a better place. I still cry and think about you all the time. I have not forgotten about you. I promise.

October 28, 2007
Dear Steve,

I wrote a poem about you. Well, I wrote a poem to cancer telling him I hate him for what he did to you. But it's over now because you are in heaven and cancer can't hurt us any more. Jesus is stronger. The victory of heaven is stronger than any sickness. . .The Final Victory

> Unannounced you come and take when you please
> You steal the sunshine, its warmth turns to ice
> All hope is lost, a door without a key
> Life is a gamble when you roll the dice
> The sky turned black as my cries went unheard
> Such pain you bring no one can be prepared
> Sorrow took my joy

> *Silence took my words*
> *Our home grew dark, we only felt despair*
> *Looking in his eyes I see shades of gray*
> *A good man he doesn't deserve to die*
> *I beg and plead for you to let him stay*
> *You killed my Dad and left me here to cry*
> *But, Cancer your pain has lost its power*
> *My Dad's in Heaven this very hour*

I watched your funeral on video yesterday. I hated that day! I hated having to go up on stage in front of all those people. I don't remember what they said while we were up there. I don't remember any of the funeral except we had to go up there and I hated it. I remember one other thing — Makena sat by me, put her hand on my shoulder and whispered to me "It's okay, Sara, don't cry. It's okay." I was so big compared to her, but I was curled up in a little ball sobbing, crying and she — a little five-year-old — was comforting me. That's it — that is all I remember.

As I watched the video, I watched Makena the whole time, she was perfect. She was trying to sing along with the hymns, she was looking at your pictures — smiling and singing. When we had to go up to the front, she made everyone laugh. I watched her so close because I wanted to see if she really came over to me or if I was just creating a memory. And then I saw it. I was sitting on stage with my face buried in my knees and she put her hand on me, looked down at my face and said something to me and I looked back at her. Just the way I remembered.

I looked so broken, I couldn't even walk by myself. I was trying so hard not to feel the pain, trying so hard to make it stop, to fight it, to go back where it came from that I wasn't even present at your funeral. Before I watched the video, I was mostly thinking how I would regret when I saw your casket on stage. When I watched the video, I didn't even remember your casket was not at the funeral. I didn't even remember that! Why didn't I remember anything? I had no clue about the white cloth, the Tootsie Rolls, or that Brenda sang, nothing — only Makena loving me even though I hated her. I hated her, I was so mean to her, but she just loved me so much.

Watching this video, I realized she was beautiful and I am so happy that she is alive and was born into my life. I have never quite felt the way I did watching her just perfect and sitting there singing praise to God, looking at a photo of you.

I have done a lot of horrible things to Mom and Makena and they both still love me, I don't know how. I was mean to a little girl, hating her before she should have ever been shown hate. I gave her no reason to love me, but she wouldn't go away. I tried to push her away by being mean, hating, yelling at her, but she kept coming back to me with more love. She still loves me "more than I love myself" is what she says. And you know what, she's probably right. She does love me more than I love myself. Thank you for her.

You would be so proud of this family if you were here. Mom is amazing! I have no clue how she is so strong or how she gets up every day without you, but she does and she smiles and does more with each day than I ever could. She is living her life dream — through so much hurt, God showed her to her purpose. That woman has more strength, love, determination and forgiveness in her than any other person on this planet. I would have never loved me or taken me back, but she did, over and over and over. Somehow I finally changed, but I put her through 21 years of hell and she is still standing tall. Plus, her parents, Bill, Amanda, you dying, I don't know how she is still so strong. Will you please tell Jesus thank you for giving her so much strength and thanks so much for giving her to me!

Thank you for choosing to be my Dad. I didn't really make your life all that joyful, but you still chose to stay. You chose to love me when it would have been easier not to. Thank you. Thank you for giving me the only thing I ever wanted — a Dad. I love you and thank you for being MY Dad! Have a perfect day in heaven.

Love,
Sara

Sara and I had been on quite the journey together, but through the grace of God, we both lived through it. It was the beginning of a new year, four years without Steve. Sara decided that on this particular Daddy Day, she wanted to celebrate both me and Steve, because we "just seemed to go together." She wrote the following for me...

Monday, January 28, 2008 2:51 AM
Happy Daddy Day, My Beautiful Mother!!!
I LOVE YOU
Have a Fabulous Day Blessed In Every Way
You are the very best Mom a girl could ask for!
Today I hope you experience the love, peace, hope and joy from the Lord!
Remember Steve today and all the amazing things he taught us...
COOKING
POKODOT
WINE
PECKING ORDER
NICE THINGS
VACATION
BASKETBALL
DETAILS
HISTORY
READING
FAMILY
LOVE
MAKENA
BUTTERED POPCORN
EDUCATION
CALM TEMPER
GENTLE SOUL
HOW TO SHOOT A FREE THROW
GOD
STRENGTH
SORROW
TO SURVIVE
HOLD ON TO FAMILY

PEACE
WISDOM
THERE IS MORE TO LIFE
GOD IS IN CONTROL
FORGIVENESS
COURAGE TO FACE EACH DAY

Steve taught us so much when he was on earth and even more when he went to heaven.

I LOVE YOU

You are so brave and so strong, working so hard to make sure we are all taken care of.

I don't know how you do it, except through God.

Mom, it is through you that I feel God's unconditional love. The love the Bible talks about is the love I feel from you.

God has a plan for our lives, we just have to hold on tight and do His will.

I love you so much and I am so glad I was chosen by God to come from your womb and be your daughter.

HAPPY DADDY DAY! YOU ARE THE BEST!
LOVE, SARA

February 28, 2008

Hi Mom, Happy Daddy Day! I wrote this for you today…

Pillar of Strength, Beckon on Hope, Endless Love
Strong like statues of Ancient Greece
You stand tall and magnificent, radiating strength for all to see
Your Hope in life shines brighter every day
Bright like a lighthouse in the night we look to you
To Love brings utmost joy and deepest sorrow
Still you choose to Love
This is your Strength that brings Hope for tomorrow.

I love you Mom,
Happy Daddy Day
Sara

March 28, 2008

Today is your special day again! Happy Daddy Day, Steve!

Boy do I miss you and hope that you can see how amazing life is going for the Patterson women! I love Mom so much and I am so proud of her too! She is the strongest person I have ever met and her strength is definitely from the Lord. All her hard work is pulling through! She followed her dreams and they are finally coming through! I love her! You will never believe this and I never told her but she is my best friend. Out of everyone in the world, I most enjoy being around her. She believes in me and listens to all my life stuff and I feel better once we talk. We laugh and have fun. It is like we are great friends. She loves me and Amanda and Makena so much. I can honestly say I LOVE HER!

I don't understand love, because it just hurts so damn bad. Mom loves me unconditionally. She never stopped. She never left me even though I hurt her so bad over and over and over. She never left me. I can finally see — that is love. I look at my Mom loving me and see God loving me. God isn't going to leave me like my biological Dad or all the other guys I thought I loved. He is not going to die and leave me behind. I see God in Mom, opening His arms — time after time. I have hurt Him, but He always says, I forgive you, Sara, I love you. Just like Mom. I see it now and never want to hurt her again.

I look at her life and it breaks my heart that she is alone without you every night. She truly loves you and misses you. I hate that she is alone with no one there to hold her and love her. I know she is strong, I just wish there was some way you didn't have to die.

Your pictures are starting to look so outdated. I am scared you are slipping into the past. Makena doesn't really remember you, and I still don't tell people you're dead. Makena is smart, like you. She loves to read and do science. She is crazy good on the computer and loves electronics, like cell phones and iPods. She is growing up. She is eight years old, 4'11" and wears a size 9 in women's shoes! I like hanging out with her. We play games and watch TV. I have noticed she loves movies where girls find their dads and reunite. I see her connecting to them. She doesn't know why they are her favorite movies, but I think it connects her to you.

I am a junior in college now and I still have good grades. I don't love school, but I am glad I am here. I struggle with keeping friendships or even wanting to be around most people. I do keep busy in my room though. I have my own company now: www.blessingjar.com. On Valentine's Day I made a present for Mom, and now the whole world wants one. I took a candle jar and decorated it with purple ribbon and hearts. Then I got quotes and printed it out on cool paper, cut them up, and put them in the jar. So Mom could have her own Blessing Jar. She loved it and showed her Bible Study friends and now I make and sell them full time. Mom got me a website and customers and all I have to do is decorate. I love it! It is fun and creative — a hobby for me that makes money! Mom sells them and does all the money part, I just get to have fun, pretty cool, huh.

So, how is heaven? Perfect I would guess. I know you are probably busy worshipping Jesus, doing heavenly things, but don't forget to be watching out for Mom and us because we still miss you. I miss you. Oh, don't worry; Polka dot and Ella (our dogs) have taken responsibility to protect us in the house from anything that moves. So I know we are safe with their ferocious barks and all. And if you are not too busy, Amanda could use some love and attention. Her job is putting her on probation and she can't lose this job! She does not listen to Mom, so maybe she might listen to you. Thanks.

Well, I hope you are having a fabulous day, blessed in every way!
I love you,
Sara

CHAPTER FORTY-ONE
Talking To God in New Zealand

It was not time that made grief better; it was the constant wrestling with what to do with the pain, where to put it so that it would not ruin my life. That seemed to give grief a purpose. Like breadcrumbs from Hansel and Gretel, each moment spent with grief seemed to lead to somewhere else. One breadcrumb, one grief experience at a time — each one leading me to someplace I had never been. One of those places was New Zealand.

Hi Babe,

It is very early in the morning in New Zealand. I am sitting in my hotel room, looking out into the dark sky. Our little women are on an airplane flying around the world to join me today, your day, on Daddy Day. Ken and I will pick them up at the airport in a few hours. We will spend a couple of weeks here, me working and the girls having the time of their life — I hope!

This hotel, this New Zealand view, working here, spending time with amazing people, it all seems normal. That is how different our lives have become. I never dreamed of coming to New Zealand. Yet God has brought me here and now I am able to bring our little women here, wow, God is good.

I am learning how little I know about the life God has planned for me. I struggle to grasp the unfamiliar settings that He seems to make feel familiar. I wake up scared. I pray. I promise God I will trust Him. I beg Him to take good care of me and our little women. He blesses me with morning light, busy days, and simple nights that occupy my fearful mind. The day ends and He has been with me every minute, and for that I give great thanks, close my eyes, and drift off to sleep.

This morning has specialness about it. I don't know if it is the anticipation of the girls arriving or if it is just the simple quiet time that God and I are spending together. I like the story He is revealing to me. It warms my heart. It is about the three of us. And today, it all seems to make sense. He whispers to me. . .

Remember October 2003

You and Steve were in Athens, Greece, attending an International Sports Ministry conference. It was the evening worship service. You were singing praise songs with people from around the world. Out of the corner of your eye, you saw tears streaming down Steve's cheeks. You reached for his hand, a familiar touch that connected your hearts. He whispers, "I feel like I have come home. The sound of men singing, worshiping God in so many different languages, comforts me. I had lost my way over the years and at this moment I feel like God has found me and brought me home." You worshiped, you prayed, you gave thanks to be in My presence, it was a night that meant something in your story. Sitting behind you was a guy from New Zealand, Ken Youngson. He noticed you, but you did not notice him.

Remember March 2005

You were in Florida, attending another International Sports Ministry conference. You were alone. Steve had died eight months earlier. You were having lunch with a group of people from Egypt. They were very interested in the Sports Life Coaching work you were doing in the States. They were asking you questions faster than you could give them answers. You felt overwhelmed; your heart ached for Steve. Ken Youngson joined your conversation. He diverted some of the questions, and you were able to regroup. Lunch ended. You and Ken agreed to talk again about the work you were doing. Days passed. You were miserable. You wished you had not come to the conference. Ken connected with you again. He asked you to come to New Zealand and share Sports Life Coaching with his organization, Quantum Sports. You both agreed to pray about it.

Remember May 2005

You received an email from Ken. He wanted to continue your conversations about you going to New Zealand. You agreed to pray about it. You had no desire to go — you did not want to leave your little women and go around the world to share sports life coaching with rugby players. You had never even seen a rugby game. A couple days passed until you were brave enough to talk to Me about it all. You asked Me what I thought about the idea. I said "Just go." You thought, yeah right — just go, no way. You asked Me to give you more information. You let Me know that it felt too big to go to New Zealand, too much of a risk, too far away from your little women. I said again, "Just go." Terrified, you knew I wanted you to go. You wished I would give you more than "Just go" but that was all I shared with you.

Remember June 2005

You emailed Ken a novel of questions. You thought if you made it difficult on him to have you, he would give up on the idea. You could then justify that you had been obedient to My words of "Just go," but it didn't work out. Ken answered every question. The two of you booked a date for you to begin working with Quantum Sports.

Remember November 2005

You spent two weeks working with Ken at Quantum Sports in New Zealand.

You left your little women. You did what I asked you to do. Together we were able to change lives. Together we made a difference. You survived. Your little women survived.

Remember August 2006

You went back to New Zealand and spent two more weeks working with Ken. We were able to do more work together. I kept you safe. I kept Amanda and Makena safe while you were away. You were able to take Sara with you to begin her certification to become a Sports Life Coach.

Remember September 2006

You and Ken began working hand-in-hand implementing Sports Life Coaching to all sports in New Zealand.

Remember Today, July 28, 2007

Sara and Makena are on their way to join you. Their lives will change today. They will see life differently because you have trusted Me. You are becoming stronger day by day. Your story is important to Me. Your life means everything to me. I love you and your little women.

Remember Jeremiah 29:11

"I know the plans I have for you," I declare, "plans to prosper you and not to harm you, plans to give you hope and a future."

The dark sky is opening up to the morning sun. It is time to go to the airport.

Thank you, God, for sharing the sunrise with me. Thank you for loving me, for protecting me, for guiding me, for holding me when I have felt so alone. I thank you for giving me the courage to "Just go." You have blessed me and my little women in ways I will only know and understand when I get to see you and Steve again.

That's all for now, Babe, I am off to the airport to pick up our little women ... oh, New Zealand will never be the same.

Here's to being connected — in the USA, in New Zealand, and in heaven!

I Love you,

C

CHAPTER FORTY-TWO
Cupcakes and Philanthropy

The following details another Hansel and Gretel moment that came from just following life's breadcrumbs. Steve had been gone six years, and there were still moments when he seemed to be sitting right beside us.

July 28, 2010
Hi Babe,

You would be proud of me. I have booked a trip to New York for this year's Daddy Day Adventure. Because the girls are getting older, growing up, and Amanda and Sara are going their separate ways, Makena and I have decided that we will go on a Daddy Day Adventure every July 28th. She gets to pick the adventure and I get to figure out how to do it and pay for it — what a deal! New York City was first on her wish list. Pretty special, since I came to New York City the first time with you.

Here is how our Daddy Day Adventures works. Makena picks the location, and then I get to work figuring out all the details. This used to be the way you did it for me. I got to tell you where I wanted to go, and then for months you worked to book every detail to make every trip, oh so special for me. I used to think I could not do this but I am stepping into my life without you, figuring out what I can and cannot do. You have taught me well and I can do this. . .I can do anything for our little women!

For me, the mission of our Daddy Day Adventures is for Makena to get to know you. For her to learn something new about you, for her to understand who you were and what you wanted for her, for her to gain an understanding of what you stood for and what our family stands for today. I think about how I can weave you into every day and yet keep it simple enough to speak to her eleven-year-old heart. It is a combination of both of you. I want it to be fun, she is all about fun, and I want her to learn something too, because you, my dear, were a teacher of life.

We landed in Baltimore, Maryland today. We are going to spend a couple days with the Matt family. They are very special to me, someone you did not even know. Kathy and I became friends when we both worked at Arizona State University. She left a year ago to take the job as Dean of the College of Health Sciences at the University of Delaware. We have shared lots of passions—our work, our love for our girls, and it has grown into a friendship. She worked her way through college as a baker. She loves to make super fancy cakes and fun cupcakes. We have gotten our girls together several times to make cupcakes and fun craft projects. Because you and Makena shared a passion for cooking together, this was the closest I could get to incorporating that shared loved. So, we started our Daddy Day with her family.

Makena loves sweets and roller-coasters. Something I don't think you were around long enough to experience. I, my dear, do not love roller-coasters but am happy to indulge in the sweets with her. So this leg of our adventure combines her love of sweets and roller-coasters. Kathy and I took all the girls (she has two daughters, older than Makena) to Hershey World. We stopped at all the cupcake bakeries along the way to sample each baker's masterpiece. It was a wonderful couple of days and a perfect way for me to work my way into taking Makena to New York City.

Kathy drove us to Princeton for our next leg of the adventure. We stopped in Philadelphia for a quick lunch and a history lesson. Makena, just like you, loves history. We toured the Liberty Bell Museum and then Betty Ross's home. What a fascinating story — what a woman — amazing what she did so long ago — certainly was a pioneer for women of today. We finished our day at the Robert Wood Johnson Foundation. We said our good-byes to Kathy as she passed our bags on to Joe Marx.

David Colby was waiting for us at the Foundation. It was late in the afternoon on Friday, so everyone had gone home, but he had waited for us. I had asked him if he would meet Makena and share the story of how he met you and why he created the Steve Patterson Sports Philanthropy Award. He greeted us and gave us a tour of the Foundation. We passed the main lobby and there in a glass case was your Award. Makena said, "We have one of those at home." She knew nothing of the details about this award other than the fact that a couple times a year I left on a trip to give out your award. She was old enough now to begin to understand your award — what it was and why you were worthy of an amazing Foundation like the Robert Wood Johnson Foundation, investing in creating an award in your honor. I wanted her to know the story behind the award.

We ended up in David's office and he began to tell the story of how he met you. I love hearing these stories; it makes me feel connected to you. I love that you are not forgotten. I love that you touched David in such a way that years after you are gone he is able to sit in his office and talk to your daughter about you — who you were to him and what you stood for as a man of great character. Makena listened. I think she liked the cupcake tastings better. But I love these moments, because I know your daughter is learning about you, is getting to know the man that I loved, the man that was her Daddy.

After our time with David, Joe Marx had agreed to take us to dinner. We ventured into the college town of Princeton and found our way to a wonderful Italian restaurant. Eileen, his wife, joined us and we spent the evening sharing stories. It was not long before Joe and Makena were off on their own private adventure — laughing, making funny faces, telling each other silly jokes. Makena liked him, there was something special about him, and her heart knew it. I watched them together and I knew that you were present. Wow, how could this be, that years earlier, you met Joe. You worked with him for a couple of months. You died. He worked with David to create an award in honor of you, and then many years later, he was blessing your daughter with love. It was a very special day and a wonderful night — all in celebration of you, my dear. Pieces of things that you started years earlier coming together to add to the pages of your daughter's story.

We ended our night with a scoop of ice cream and Joe dropping us off at our hotel. We would take the train to New York City in the morning.

The next morning, we waited at the train station to continue our adventure into the city. Both of us not sure what the heck we were doing and both of us wishing we were hanging out with Joe instead. As usual, I pretended that I had it all under control; I guess I learned that from you, my dear. When Makena would look at me with those huge eyes, scared but yet wanting to be brave, I would assure her that everything was going to be okay. Wow, I sure hoped I could deliver on that promise. Thank goodness you and God are committed to hanging out with me, because between the three of us, we seem to be raising quite the amazing daughter.

I wish you could have seen Makena's eyes when we walked outside from the train station and into New York City. It was a moment I will never forget. She stood there, not sure what to do — wanting to be excited because she had been dreaming of this moment, but totally overwhelmed. People bumping into us, the noise of the city, the grit, the smell, so New York but so not what she had envisioned. We took a cab to our hotel. . .let the City Adventure begin!

The two things on the top of Makena's list were to see the Lion King and to go to Cake Boss's Bakery in New Jersey. When I had gone online to buy tickets for the Lion King, they were so expensive that they would take all of our budget. So we had talked about taking a risk and waiting until we got to the city to try and get cheaper tickets the day of. Today was that day of, and I was so hoping I could find tickets for us.

We went to the concierge, and he told us they were sold out. Makena melted. She hates taking risks, and I had convinced her to go for it. She started to cry and told me that is why she hates taking risks, it never works out. The concierge told us we could try waiting in line for tickets. Perfect, we headed right out to find that line. We were the first people in line — three hours to curtain call. We were both tired from the excitement of getting to the city and welcomed the quiet of just the two of us sitting on the floor at the box office. We shared stories of our adventure so far. I told her about the times you and I spent in the city. And then fifteen minutes before the show started, they called our name — they had two seats in the fourth row. Thank you, God! Better seats than we could have ever afforded to buy, totally worth the wait in line.

We spent the next couple of days seeing the sights and soaking in every aspect of the Big Apple. On our last day in the city, Monday, I had planned to take a cab to Cake Boss's bakery. I figured it would be less crowded on Monday. We arrived at 9am. There was a line around the block to get into the bakery. You have got to be kidding me. I looked at Makena — she knows I hate waiting in line, much less for a bakery — she begged me to stay. We did. We got in line, and four hours later, we made it into the bakery. Cake Boss is one of her favorite shows. She watches that show and the food channel just like you used to — makes me think of you as I watch her enjoying all those cooking shows.

Once we were in the bakery, one of the people on the show came downstairs. I asked him if he would take a picture with Makena. He agreed, and she snuggled under his arm for the shot — a huge smile and a magical twinkle in her eyes. As we made our way out of the very crowded bakery, she was quiet. I asked her what she thought of it all. She said that when she was taking her picture, she told him that he was her favorite and then he told her that she was his favorite. She felt so special. The whole way back in the taxi she looked at that picture and kept telling me about how he said she was his favorite too. Another very special life moment.

It had been an amazing Daddy Day Adventure. . .we were both ready for home sweet home.

With all my love,

C

CHAPTER FORTY-THREE
Road Trip, Tears, and Love

Thanksgiving, 2010
Hi Babe,

The girls and I are driving to Artesia (New Mexico) for Thanksgiving. It has been years since all the families have been together. The girls are all growing up and have real jobs now, so making time for cousins and family has been difficult. Dad had a kidney transplant in August and had lots of complications. We thought for sure we were going to lose him, but as usual, God had a different plan. Dad was finally out of the hospital and healthy again, so all of us made it our mission to spend Thanksgiving together. The girls and I have a ten-hour road trip ahead of us, so I decided this would be a good time to tell them about this book draft. I hope that we can read it on the way so they can let me know what they think of it and make any changes they want before I pursue getting it published.

8:00 a.m. Wednesday Morning

We packed the car and headed south to New Mexico. It has been a long time since we were all together because Amanda hates to travel and never goes on family trips with us. This trip was an exception because it was to see Papa (my Dad). The girls know that every road trip I have books on tape for us to listen to and usually some big project I want to share with them. I always take advantage of having them captive for any length of time. They know this and are used to it.

Our trip started out in the usual way — a bit of catch-up chatter, a few music CDs, a stop for a snack, and then we settled in for hours and miles of "are we there yet." This was my cue. I stared to share with the girls that I had been keeping all of our writings to you and our journal entries from Daddy Day in a book. I was hoping they would read the book and let me know what they thought because I was considering pursuing publishing it. They were curious. Okay, let's read the book.

Amanda became our book on tape. Mile after mile, she read page after page of our life story. Oh, babe, I can't tell you what it was like watching our little women listen to our love story. They hung on every word. They loved hearing about you and me and our love for each other. They waited in anticipation to see if I wrote about them on the next page. Makena was very quiet. This was all new information to her. Amanda and Sara had lived through it all, but Makena did not remember much of this. I know the pages were filling in blank pages in her life story. She had memories, but they were fragmented. She had been too young to capture all the details. And then today, she was finding the words that began to lead her to all the why's she had been searching for.

I watched in pure awe as each daughter had tears streaming down her cheeks. They were speechless. They had no idea I had documented all our pain, in such detail. And then the chapter came, Time to Say Good-Bye. Through sobs of tears, Sara said, "Stop reading! Maybe if we don't read it, it won't happen." Six and a half years after you died, we hope if we just don't say it, it won't be true. But I have said it, and it is true.

We drove for a while in silence, and then Sara said, "Keep reading." What happened in the next few minutes is something I will never forget. Locked in a car, somewhere between Arizona and New Mexico, our three precious little women and I faced our truth — you had died. We all cried — the first time we had faced this together. And then, through the tears, Sara said, "Keep reading! We know it gets better!"

We arrived in Artesia, emotionally wiped out, but happy to be with family. None of us talked about the book. We enjoyed the time with cousins and extended family. We ate. We talked. We spent time together. My brother took Makena out to the dirt roads to teach her to drive — oh the joys of living on a ranch. She also got to drive a four-wheeler, work in the cow pins, and get all dirty — not her favorite thing to do, being the city girl that she is.

The days passed, and then on Saturday morning, we loaded up for our road trip home. I don't think we had gone more than a few miles when Makena asked Amanda to keep reading. She took out the book and continued to read about our lives. It was a very special time. There was a moment when Amanda read a poem I had written to you, and Makena asked, "Who wrote that?" and Amanda said, "Mom!" She was silent. It made me cry. I knew she was getting to know me in a very different way. I had let the girls into our world. I was not just Mom anymore, I was someone that had feelings, someone that hurt just as bad as they did, and missed you so much. There were times when Amanda would pause and tell me how impressed she was with my writing. It touched my heart to share our story with our little women.

We finished the book about the same place we started reading it — a few hours from home. We had gone through boxes of tissue, cried for hours, laughed at silly stories, but most important, we had accepted our story. We got In-N-Out Burger for dinner, said a special "We love you, Steve," and then finished the drive home.

We unpacked the car, said good-bye to Sara (she is living on her own now), all so happy to be home again. Makena was very quiet. After a few minutes, she asked me if we could watch home videos. We pulled out the box labeled "Makena" and snuggled up on the couch. We watched hours of you two doing simple things together. We watched you play in the ocean, we watched you cook pancakes together, we watched you read her a story, and we watched you love her. It was so sweet. So powerful to hear your voice. And then the tapes were over, and we did not have any more footage with you. Your story with Makena had ended.

With all my love,
C

CHAPTER FORTY-FOUR
The Gift of Friendships

December 2, 2010
Hi Babe,

I am in Coronado this weekend, celebrating another birthday without you. It is a good birthday though. You would be so proud of all your little women, including me. God is taking great care of us, and most importantly, I am so proud to say that we are letting Him. I think we have truly learned to surrender — wow, seven years of hell to say those words.

I am sitting at a small white desk, sliding glass doors open, and the most beautiful view of nothing but ocean and blue skies, yum, God is so good! I am here, in a place that I have always dreamed of being. I did not know the address or how I was ever going to get here, but I am here and I am happy. It is a kind of happiness that I didn't know existed, a peace in my heart that feels like nothing I have ever experienced.

I am alone but don't feel lonely. I like hanging out with me; it gives me time to talk to you and God. Our little women have gotten used to me going away for my birthday, and this one is even more special since they know I am working to finish this book. I don't know if these pages will ever get from my computer to the world, or if God even wants that to happen, but I can tell you, these pages have brought such healing to each one of us, and for that I give great thanks. It is our story, we have lived through each page, and by saving them, I can remember all the simple moments when God has taken our hands and held on tight, as we all wanted to give up.

I am staying at Jim and Carol's place; they have it up for sale, so I am not sure if I will ever get to come back. Maybe that is why it is feeling so special to me. I know it has been a blessing to them for years, and now they are ready to let someone else experience the gift of life by the sea. The first time you brought Makena to the beach, was this one — in Coronado. I think it may have even been my birthday because the two of you packed up for the weekend and came over here to give me a weekend to myself. I have the picture of her playing in the sand with the Hotel Del in the background. We never came back here as a family.

The first time Makena and I came here was a couple years ago. Jim and Carol gave us the weekend as a gift. Wow, what a gift of love they have been to our family. Not only have they blessed us with weekends with a view, but they have loved us through some of the toughest years. Last year, Makena asked Jim if he would be her Daddy G — her Daddy sent from God. She has wanted a Daddy so much, and all I can give her is that she has an amazing Daddy, he just lives in heaven. She always honors my words but continues to tell me she so wants a Daddy here on earth. So she asked Jim — got to love a kid that goes for what she wants. Jim was so gracious about it and has stepped right up to be her Daddy G! It is just their special relationship. He calls her, they chat about life, he takes her for ice cream, they hang out at the Apple store talking electronics. . .it's cute. I don't know which one enjoys it more, Makena or Jim.

Carol and I have become great friends. She has walked beside me through my letting go and going forward years. She knows my pain as a mom who watches her children cry out for things we cannot give them; she knows my wants as a woman who cherishes love; she knows my desire to be the woman God created me to be. The list of how she has blessed me goes on and on.

When Sara graduated from college, I asked Carol and the women in our Bible Study if they would help me throw her an amazing party. Oh my goodness, babe, Sara got the party of her dreams – every detail was perfect! You know I was no help because the party that these "over the top" blessed women put together was bigger and better than anything I could have even imagined, so impressive. As a family, we all went to Sara's graduation. Once we walked out the door, Carol and her "Let's Change Someone's Life" team of women walked in our door and life changed.

Dozens and dozens of flowers, amazing food, a cake that seemed to be delivered to the wrong address — it was meant for royalty, not our simple home graduation party — all became the props in a beautiful picture that was soon going to become the perfect refection of the breathtaking young woman Sara had become. We were only gone a few hours, but what these amazing women did to our home was more like open heart surgery. They had taken all their gifts that God had blessed them with and showered them on our family. It was so much more than making our home beautiful; they created a gorgeous place to let go of the pain and welcome new beginnings.

Diploma in hand, we pulled up to our home. It looked the same on the outside, but what happened when we opened the door was life-changing. These women had made our home look like the love we felt for each other. Sara walked into a page out of Better Homes and Garden, she was stunned. I did not even think our house had the capacity to be transformed with such elegance, beauty, and best of all, an abundance of love. It was a moment when one piece of Sara's broken heart was healed. She was experiencing the beauty and the over-the-top visions that she always dreamed of as a little girl but felt like with me as a mom, she would just have to tuck them away and pretend they didn't matter. I always knew they mattered. I just did not know how to give them to her. Enter Carol and her "Women of the Bible." What they thought was a graduation party, to us was a God Moment that we had always wanted but had given up on having. Another gift of a lifetime!

That summer, Carol asked me to help her write a Bible Study curriculum. She wanted it to be about the Women of the Bible. God could not have picked a better woman than Carol to dive into the women of the Bible's stories and make them come alive for today's women. She spent the summer getting to know these women of the Bible. She found pieces of their stories that resonated with our stories. After weeks of study, she would call me and I would join her in Coronado, to offer simple words of encouragement and cheer her on to do the next chapter. It was an amazing summer that launched an amazing fall as we taught the Study.

Now, years later, I am here writing to you. I'm finishing a draft of a book that documents our family's journey through finding love, losing love, wanting love, receiving love, but best of all beginning to understand love.

December 3
Good Morning Babe,

I smiled as I woke up to the sound of the waves crashing onto the beach. There is a chill in the air that has God's name written all over it. I am surrounded by beauty. I am alone, but I feel so loved. I spent the night last night reading from my old journals and your Bible. I always love to read your handwritten notes. Just seeing your handwriting on paper takes me to a place of pure joy. I read everything that you have written, in hopes that I might find a message from you that I have not noticed the other times

I have read your same notes. Nothing special showed up this time except that I can feel it is time to let go of reading all these old journal entries. They have served their purpose in helping me understand my pain and inch my way into my future. I am ready to let them go.

I am sitting here, wearing cozy purple pajamas bottoms that Sara bought me for my birthday, a sweatshirt from UCLA, and Makena's Uggs that she has outgrown and passed down to me. If I had something on of Amanda's, I would be wearing the whole family. I love having you all with me in your very unique ways!

Sara gave me her journal of all the letters she has written to you, so that I could include them in this book. I sat down and begin to type her words from each page. I have not stopped crying. Oh my goodness, I had no idea she felt the way she did. I knew she hated me. I knew how miserable she was. I knew how sad she was. I knew how much she missed you, but to read her words — her very tender, raw words to you, the only Daddy she has ever known — felt like I was handed another dose of love. This time in a small black journal, with the words Dear Dad written on every page.

With all my love,
C

December 11
Hi Babe,

I am still celebrating my birthday. You know how much I love to celebrate all month! Bob and Paula took me to dinner at Tarbell's tonight. They arrived a bit earlier than me and had a fabulous bottle of wine waiting for us to enjoy. We were seated at a table for four, and as I began to take my seat next to Paula, she said "No, sit here — next to Bob." I sat down and felt the love of two wonderful friends as we dove into catching up and toasting to all that life has to offer. The night was filled with delicious food, fabulous wine, heart-healing laughter, tears, joy, and all the really important things in life.

As we shared our stories, not a moment went by that I did not have the view of the empty table right behind us. It was the table where Michelle, Sara, and I sat having dinner the last night you were here on earth. The guys from your Bible Study had come to the house to host their meeting in our bedroom, so you could be a part of it. Sara and I had nothing left in us. The pain of what was happening was catching up, and we were not sure we could handle it. Where better to go than Tarbell's, one of our favorite hangouts. The image of the three of us was picture perfect in my mind. I remembered us making simple conversation but me hearing nothing except the deafening sound of you gasping for breath, which I knew was happening at home. We nourished our souls and prepared for what was next, whatever that meant. Little did we know that next was going to be tougher than anything we could have imagined.

Six and half years later, I am sitting at a different table, the three of us — a different three, different stories, oh so different circumstances, and yet there you are, your memory joining me. I wish you knew Bob and Paula, but I know you do — you probably sent them to me. Thank you.

As we order dinner and sip our wine, we lose ourselves in conversation as we indulge in the stories of life — how business is going, what we are dreaming of doing next, our God Moments, the latest books we have read. We have learned that simple words, delivered at simple moments, can show up in powerful ways — days, months, and years after they have been spoken into our hearts. Bob and Paula are those kinds of friends to me. They speak into my heart. They are never too far away to pick me up when the days seem too difficult. They are always around to celebrate the simple joys of friendship as we muddle through the not so simple things that life brings to us each day. We are interrupted by Mark Tarbell stopping by to wish me a Happy Birthday. He knows how special his place is to me. As Mark left, I shared with Bob and Paula how he made soup for you every night when you were sick. They don't know you, but they know you through me. It seems as though all the places we go together, I have a story of us. They listen, they care, they have learned to love you from far away, yet they too have honored your place in my heart.

Dessert comes and there is one little candle, lit, just waiting for my birthday wish. I don't think that one little candle could possibly hold all my birthday wishes, but I am totally up for giving it a try. I make my wishes. Blow out the candle. And as I sit and enjoy dessert, I feel the memories of us. This has been such a special place in our life journey. Oh the stories all those tables hold. There's the booth that we celebrated one of our biggest business deals. I can still see us so joy-filled and happy to have each other to share such a moment. We celebrated every birthday here. We sat here during tough times; searching for what to do next, hoping the comfort of our hangout would provide some answers. The private room that we had booked for dinner the night the Robert Wood Johnson Foundation staff was in town — the dinner that you were too sick to make. It was June 2004. I can remember you placing the call to the staff to let them know that you could not make it and me thinking, something is seriously wrong. And then months go by before I go back. It is another sad night. Makena and I are at home, wondering what to do with each other. You are dead, we are miserable, and Makena says, "Let's go to Tarbell's," words she heard us say so often. So she gets all dressed up, packs her princess credit card in her shiny little purse, and the two of us go out to Tarbell's. We ask for a table for two. She orders french fries and a Shirley Temple; I order a glass of wine and a comforting meal. We toast, we talk, and we feel better just being there. The bill comes, and she proudly takes out her princess credit card and treats me to dinner. Tonight, many years later, Bob and Paula are treating me to dinner. And you, my dear, have treated me to a lifetime of wonderful memories. They make me smile, they make me cry, they make me realize how powerful love is and how it lives on in ways impossible to imagine.

I arrive home from dinner around 8:30. Makena is not even home yet from one of her Christmas parties. I wait up for her, reliving all the memories served up to me tonight as I sat at that table for four. Life is good, babe. And then your little one bounces in. She is 5'7" now, 11 years old, and bubbling with you all over. She does not have a princess credit card anymore but so wishes she had a real one. We all wish for lots of things, but you, my dear, have made many of our wishes come true.

Lots of love,
C

December 12
Hi Babe,

I had lunch today, another birthday celebration, with Robin. You don't know Robin. Makena introduced me to her. We met when Abbi and Julian, Robin's daughters, became great friends with Makena. Makena was six years old, you had been gone a year. It was Robin who kept Makena when I went on my trips to be with you in Monterey. She did not know what

I was doing there. She never asked any questions. She was just there for me and Makena, the pure definition of friendship. She accepted us even when she did not know our story.

Once I returned from a trip to Monterey and Jim, Robin's husband, had spent some time with Makena showing her pictures of your UCLA basketball years. He had loved UCLA basketball and knew of you. Leave it to God to connect him to us many, many years later. A young guy with a love of basketball, listening to UCLA basketball games on the radio. Fast forward and a tall six-year-old shows up at his house for a sleepover because her mommy is on a trip, visiting her daddy's grave. He does not know her daddy. Once the girls have snuggled in for the evening, Jim asks Robin about Makena. She shares our story. "The Steve Patterson" Jim asks. Robin, not being a fan of basketball, is not quite sure what he means by that question. She and I have not spent much time talking about you as a basketball player. She only knows you as Makena's Daddy — such a God Moment.

I returned from that trip, greeted Makena with a big hug, and in her little hand was a color copy, from the Internet, of a picture of you. "Look, Mommy, Jim found a picture of Daddy playing basketball on the Internet. Jim said Daddy was a really good basketball player." I smiled, such a tender moment. And so your story continues, one friendship, one memory at a time. The girls ran off to play. Robin and Jim poured me a glass of wine, and we begin to share our stories.

Today's story is about a small, purple gift bag. Robin and her girls recently returned from their annual Thanksgiving trip to Hawaii. We both love Hawaii, and I was looking forward to hearing all the latest stories. And so she begins...she shares about how one day I am on her heart and she just keeps thinking about me. She and the girls go on a hike, and as they wind their way through the simple trails, they discover this amazing lava rock. It sits in the sea, and as it has absorbed the waves pounding against it, a heart has been carved out of the center of the rock. It is quite the famous sight, but she knew nothing about it until, unexpectedly, she and her girls discovered it. Sounds like God to me. She takes a picture for me, and as they continue their adventure, she also discovers a small lava rock in the shape of a heart. As I open the small, purple gift bag, there in a beautiful, beachy frame is the picture of this lava rock with a perfectly shaped heart in the middle of its rough, rocky shape. And on the frame, she has glued the small heart shaped rock they found. That is a perfect description of our friendship. We have made sure that each other stays connected to our heart as the waves of life pound against us.

December 13
Hi Babe,

Another birthday celebration. I so love this! Loral and I had dinner tonight. We went to a new Italian restaurant. We love to search out the new places opening and give them a try — like you and I used to do. This one is a keeper; I will have to take the girls there.

Hours passed as we shared our hearts. I told Loral all about my book and our amazing car ride to New Mexico. She gets how amazing it really was based on what we have all been through. Every chapter of grief the girls and I went through, she was there. She was the one that took my calls when I didn't think I could do it anymore. She never asked any details, she just said, "Where would you like to meet for a glass of wine?" We would meet. I would share. She would listen. We would order another glass of wine. And many hours later, I would feel strong enough to go back home and do another day without you.

I know you know all these things already because you have been with me on this journey. I wonder what you would write to me if I could get mail from heaven.

We closed the restaurant down and slowly walked to our cars. As we hugged good-bye, Loral ask me if I wrote about my "Dead People" group in the book. I laughed and told her, "No, I am not sure that is something I should include." She said, "Why not? You hated going to your Dead People group." I did hate going to that group. (My "Dead People" group is how I referred to my grief support group. And I did hate going). It was so sad to sit for hours and listen to how miserable everyone was. I did not want to be in that group. I hated that you had died and I qualified to belong to such a sad group. But I went, and month by month we all got better. I had forgotten that I usually met Loral afterwards for a glass of wine to share all that I learned from my "Dead People" group.

As we leaned against our cars, the night air fresh and crisp with a desert chill, we spoke of tender memories — ones that only she and I would know of. I had blocked most of them out of my mind, they were just too painful. But tonight, we were both strong enough to go there, and my favorite part — tonight we laughed instead of cried.

Little did you know when you handed me Loral's business card to be the attorney to represent me when you fired me, that she would end up being the one to sit with me for hours as I tried to make sense of the impossible. It was Loral whom God tapped on the shoulder, asking her to help me design your headstone. I don't remember how many versions we went through, but I do remember she was there for every sketch. I remember how I wanted to say so much on it, and she patiently helped me find just the perfect words. We ended up with Faith, Hope, Love, and the Greatest of these is Love, and then at the bottom of the cross, the words To our Harvest with two wine glasses toasting. This was a request the makers of the headstone had not had before and they kept sending me sketches of champagne glasses-no, I had to have wine glasses. Loral made sure all the details that were so important to me were always honored. She gently convinced me to make simple changes that represented what I wanted long term versus the sheer desperation I was feeling at that moment. She knew our family would look at that headstone forever, and she helped me make it perfect.

We went from designing headstones to remodeling the house. I would never have made it through all the remodeling without Loral. She was a friend that had a great knack for decorating, and she took me and the house on as her special project. There were so many days that I would have given up if it were not for her showing up and driving me to the construction warehouses to pick out a sink or a faucet, a ceiling fan, light fixtures. I didn't care at the time, but she knew I would later. She saved us from living in a Barney house, as she referred to it, because left to my own devices, I would have painted the inside and the outside of our house purple. She was tough when she needed to be and tender when I felt like there was no way I could make another decision without you.

We gave each other another hug and went our separate ways. Makena was calling. She needed help on her homework.

As I drove home, I noticed that every tough memory I was now strong enough to go back and visit had Loral with me, facing it, figuring it out, and moving on to the next one. All with a simple glass, or two, of red wine in hand — we figured it out.

As I turned the corner to come home, the song I learned in Girl Scouts many, many years ago, came to mind: "Make new friends but keep the old, some are silver and the others gold." I am so blessed to have an abundance of silver and gold. Thank you, God!

I would never have made it through losing you without the amazing cradle of love and friendship God created for me. Without my brother and his family, and all these friends, this story would have been written so differently. What a gift we are given when God brings someone so special into our lives and says, "Here is a friend that I have picked just for you. You two will need each other, and together you will be able to figure it out."

Thanks for being my best friend on earth and from heaven. And thank God for me for all the amazing friends he picked for me to share my life with, for them to know my little women, and to let us know them and their stores. Life is changing, my dear, but I know you know this because you have a different view of life now. See you someday. . .

Lots of love,

C

CHAPTER FORTY-FIVE
Our First Family Picture

December 28, 2010
Hi Babe,

The day you died, I stopped taking pictures. I went from documenting every moment of our lives, scrapbooking on the weekends, to never picking up a camera again. It was not a conscious decision. I just did not do it anymore. I guess at first, life was just too terrible. There was nothing I would even want to take a picture of and certainly nothing I wanted to put in a scrapbook. Time did go on and good things did happen, but I still never wanted to take any more pictures.

The girls asked me continuously to get a family picture taken. I would agree and then somehow just not find the time to make it happen. Year after year, the Christmas cards rolled in and Makena would ask why we never sent one out. I would talk about doing one for New Year's or maybe next year, but next year never happened.

Every picture in our home has you in it. But they are beginning to look very outdated. I think it is time to change our pictures. I think it is time for me to start to document the amazing life that God is blessing us with, without you.

I have tried to stop time. I have tried to pretend that you are still present in our lives. But the pictures don't lie. You are not here anymore, and you have been gone a long time. I never wanted to take a family picture because if I took one without you in it, I would be accepting that you are gone. I accept it. We took our first family photo today. . .your day, Daddy Day.

CHAPTER FORTY-SIX
Someday...Italy

Time gets distorted once grief moves into your life. Even today, I can be as close to Steve's death as his last breath and feel as though he died just minutes ago, or it feels like he's been gone forever. I struggle to remember his touch, his voice, his presence that made me feel like I was connected to someone who loved me deeply. I never know what memory is going to show up or if someone is going to say something that triggers an emotional flashback. Time has become irrelevant. I don't spend as much time with Steve anymore. My life seems so different. Not only are Amanda and Sara grown up, but Makena is tall enough to look me right in the eye. They're still my little women, but only their tender hearts seem to be "little" anymore.

Sometimes, out of the blue, something so "Steve" shows up. It's as though he's sending us a hug from heaven. These hugs usually come through Makena — something she says or something she does makes us feel like Steve's hanging out with us. She has so much of her daddy in her spirit. Even though he was with her for only five years here on earth, they seem to know each other in a much deeper way.

Makena loves traveling just as much as Steve did. She had been asking me to take her to Italy for a couple of years, and it just seemed too big to do without Steve. And then I remembered that nothing is too big for God. So Makena and I are doing our part to get ready for our trip to Italy. We are starting to learn Italian, mapping out where we want to go, and most importantly praying for God to show us his way.

Steve, Sara, my niece Stevie, and I went to Italy for his fiftieth birthday. It was such an incredible trip. He had played basketball in Italy and had not been back since. We planned the trip for about a year, and it was defiantly a trip of a lifetime!

We stayed at Residence San Zeon in Verona. When we arrived at the train station, the owner of the Residence was there to greet us and take us to what we would call home for a week or so. As soon as he saw Steve, he recognized him—can you believe it? Well, I guess it's not too often that a 6'9" guy shows up in Italy. The owner was so excited to be hosting Steve that he rearranged our rooms and gave us a wonderful apartment. He was so proud as he escorted us to the master suite, a beautiful room with a gorgeous view and a wonderful bed with a headboard and footboard. Remember, with Steve's height, he couldn't sleep in a bed with a footboard — he wouldn't fit. We both smiled and thanked the owner for his gracious gift of such a beautiful apartment.

We all moved in, Sara and Stevie unpacking and giggling as they got to share the master suite. Steve and I found our way to the other bedroom, furnished with two twin beds — just headboards, no footboards. We pushed the twin beds together, snuggled up, and smiled as we fell between the cracks in the bed. Oh the joys of being so tall.

That trip touched our souls. Steve and I found such peace in Italy. The romance spoke to our hearts. The wine and fabulous pasta fed our spirits. The beauty and history answered questions about life that we had been searching for. Best of all, we found it all together.

We took that trip in June 1998. One year later, June 18, 1999, we were in a hospital delivery room, Steve reading the pages of *A Year in Provence* to me as I went through labor to deliver our last child, Makena. She entered the world hearing about the adventures of travel, and I do hope to show her the world, one fabulous trip at a time.

And now, twelve years later, seven years after Steve died, our daughter, Makena, longs to go to Italy. . .for Daddy Day. Maybe someday — I don't know when or how — but I'm sure Steve and Makena will figure out all the details. Maybe for her Sweet Sixteen.

I hope God has this in his plans for us.

To be continued. . .

CHAPTER FORTY-SEVEN
Forgiveness

This journey through death has taught me so much about life. I'm sorry that when I went through my divorce, I didn't have the tools or knowledge to help Amanda and Sara the same way I've helped Makena through losing her daddy. My divorce was like a death for Amanda and Sara. They lost their dad and their family, as they knew it. Going through a divorce is different from having a spouse die, but there are similarities. The biggest difference I experienced was that I didn't feel like it was my fault that Steve died. I didn't have to justify what happened to everyone or accept that I played any role in it. I could just accept help and grieve the loss of Steve and our dreams of being together. That's not the way I felt when I got divorced. I wish I had known it was okay to honor that huge loss. I wish I had felt safe enough to respect the pain instead of trying to pretend it didn't exist.

When I got divorced, I wanted to pretend that part of my story never happened, but it did, and those chapters created Amanda and Sara. By trying to edit out all the ugly details, I was sending Amanda and Sara a message that part of their story was not worth remembering. This was so not true! Every page of our life story serves a purpose.

I wish I had understood the power of grief when I went through my divorce. I wish that Amanda and Sara could have been given all the grace to grieve the loss of their biological dad, the same way Makena was able to spend years grieving the death of her daddy. All of my little women lost their daddy, but how I handled it was so different.

Amanda and Sara lived life feeling abandoned, feeling that they had done something wrong to make their mommy and daddy get a divorce. If you think about it, from a child's point of view, it does seem quite terrible that their mommy and daddy—the two people that loved each other so much, got married, and made a commitment to be together forever—would decide, one day, that they didn't love each other anymore. What could be so terrible that it makes you stop loving someone? As adults, we don't answer those questions when our children ask them. Instead, we tell them something awful about their other parent. Can you blame them for becoming confused and wondering when they're going to do something so awful that we stop loving them? What a powerful message of conditional love that teaches our children. So much pain because the person we married didn't turn out to be the person we wanted them to be or didn't give us everything we wanted them to give us.

I know that in both of my marriages I didn't turn out to be the person I wanted to be. I could blame this on my first husband because divorce is great at the blame game. I could not blame this on Steve; death does not play games.

I have learned to let go of Steve, our dreams of raising our girls, growing old together, and spending forever at the beach. I have learned to forgive Amanda and Sara's biological dad and give thanks for our brief union that created two of the most amazing blessings I have in my life today. I have learned both of these gifts — letting go and forgiveness — from my three little women. They have trusted me enough to let go of the promises I made to them that I was not able to keep. They have forgiven me for not being the mom that they wanted or for not being able to give them the life they dreamed of having. We have endured the pain of grief. We have faced our truth about our stories and made peace with all the chapters that we did not like. God is so good. He is the one that gave us the strength to do what we all felt was impossible.

I spent so many years angry at my parents for all the terrible mistakes they made — until I started editing the pages on my life as a mom. Wow, my little women have plenty to be angry with me about too. But we have done the work on our issues, forgiven each other, and have moved on to make new mistakes — together.

I did not give my parents that grace. I couldn't figure out why in the world they did the things they did. As God and I began to talk about these chapters of my life, he showed me that they did the very best they could. I started thinking about how many resources we have in our lives to work through our issues. They had none. They were not given the tools to talk about how they felt or the grace to ask questions. They were taught to figure it out on their own and speak as little as possible about their fears. It seems quite silly that my generation, which has been in therapy for years, talking about how messed up our parents made us, have an abundance of education, tools, resources, and funds — everything needed to create a perfect life — and we too are making mistake after mistake while raising our children. I realized I should leave my poor parents alone and spend that energy getting my own story right.

CHAPTER FORTY-EIGHT
Never Give Up
Where We Are Today

It has been seven years since July 28, 2004. Our family is different, but we have made peace with different. We still celebrate Daddy Day on the 28th of every month. We love our Lord Jesus with all our heart, and we know grief and pain are part of our life story.

And so today, July 28, 2011, Daddy Day, I asked the girls to write Steve a letter, to share their lives with him and reflect on their story. We spent the day together, writing, laughing, crying, talking about memories, sharing dreams, but most of all grateful to be moving on. We finished our day with dinner at Tarbell's. It was special, it was different, but it was us. Aaron, Sara's fiancé, joined us, and most of our conversations were about our future, not our past. I know that Steve would be happy about that.

Amanda's Love Letter. . .she didn't want to write one. Some things never change. Amanda always does things her way and in her own time. I'm proud of her and where her journey has taken her. She's still living at home, but Makena is working very hard on helping her with her "moving out" plan. We have a peaceful relationship. We are learning to respect each other for who we really are instead of who we wish we were for each other. Not a day goes by that Amanda does not teach me something, either about myself or about the world she lives in. Our days are not always easy, and we struggle with expectations and disappointments, but we are okay with that now. We get that it's part of life. I have no idea what the future holds for Amanda, but I do know that every day God holds her and leads her toward the life he has created just for her. For that I give great thanks!

This year, twenty-eight years after the world was blessed with Amanda, she has found her voice. She found peace with her story and through SAARC has been able to find the words and language to share it, in hopes of helping other families navigating through their autism experience. Here is her speech that she gave to the SAARC Grandparents group. By reading her writings, you can step into Amanda's world and see that she makes sense of it by documenting facts. She tells her story and lives her life in a very structured way. It is change and the unexpected that leave her lost. It is wanting emotion rather than facts that can make her seem disconnected, but she is probably more connected to her heart and soul than most of us.

> Hi. I am Amanda.
>
> I graduated from Arizona Christian University, formerly Southwestern Bible College, with an Associates in General Studies degree in May of 2006.
>
> I got involved in SAARC in early 2008. My mom had me fill out the paperwork. I knew I had autism but didn't want to admit it. Also, I really didn't want to go to SAARC. My mom made me go and I went along to make her happy. So my mom and I walked into SAARC and Erin Dunham talked to us and showed us around. After seeing the place, I thought it might be okay but I still wasn't happy.
>
> I started out at SAARC volunteering so that they could get to know me and I could get to know them. One of the volunteer things I did was Culinary Works. It was for job training. Erin Dunham worked with me and one other client along with the chefs of the soup that we made. SAARC is now selling the soup at a Farmer's Market on Wednesday nights.
>
> Also, I did some of the classes and other social opportunities that they offer. One of my favorites that I still love to go to is Monday night out. It is always a lot of fun. It has different themes, and we play games in groups, have dinner and free time at the end.
>
> While I was doing that, I had a person helping me look for a job environment I would be interested in working in. She went with me to informational interviews.
>
> After that, I broke my ankle as soon as we set my goal of looking for a cleaning job in mid-2009. I broke my ankle in September. By December 2009, I was able to start looking for a job and applying for jobs.
>
> Erin Dunham started out as my job coach. She ended up getting me the job that she had in mind, working at a laundry mat.
>
> Erin helped me fill out the application and do my resume to go to the job and apply. It was the same day that they were going to do my interview.
>
> So before we went, Erin Dunham had me do some mock interviews. It is where she and staff at SAARC — some that I knew well and some that I didn't know too well — interviewed me and asked me questions that I was going to be asked in the interview or that could have been asked.
>
> I went to the interview, and they hired me on the spot, which made me so happy that I got a job.

When I started working there, Erin Dunham was working with me, training me at the job. She showed me how to do the job that I was supposed to do and encouraged me every day to do something better or taught me something new about the job that I needed to know.

That job ended up not working out because there was a staff switch. That happened right after the New Year of 2010.

After that, Erin Onacki ended up taking over as my job coach. She worked with me again on looking for jobs. So she went to look and speak to the bosses of Advantage Mail. It is a warehouse that mails out the promotional mail that you get.

She got the application from them, we filled it out, and she turned it in for me.

When I got the call for the interview, I let Erin Onacki know. She did have people after that do mock interviews with me again.

The interview was the day after my birthday, and they told me after the interview that I got the job and that they wanted me to start the following Monday. I was so happy to hear I got a job.

Erin went with me to work and worked with me the first few weeks I was working there. She helped me get the place so I could clean it when she wasn't there.

She also helped my bosses to know how to help me at work if I needed help after Erin was no longer there. Also, she worked with me on social skills with and around my bosses and co-workers.

My 1st day of working at Advantage Mail was Monday, February 15th. Since I got there a little early, they let me watch what was going on. I thought it looked like a different place to work. I have never seen so many machines for mail.

I remember Erin Onacki was a little late getting there that day. One of my bosses — I don't remember if it was Julie or Patti — introduced me to everyone until Erin got there. When Erin got there, my boss walked me through what they wanted me to do every day. I thought there would be no way I would be able to do all of that and that the warehouse will probably never even look clean or near clean at all.

I was nervous and scared if I didn't or couldn't do all those things that they would fire me.

Erin Onacki helped me get to it where the place looked manageable to clean and started to really help me learn what supplies were what.

One thing that isn't work related that we have at work is a treadmill. My bosses encourage me to do the treadmill, and when I take a break from doing it for a day or two, I feel guilty but I do need those breaks.

My counselor and I have heard other people say by doing the treadmill that it helps to lose weight and with my anxiety that I have, which is not much because I am very happy with what is going on in my life.

I have the same schedule every week for days off and times I work, and there are really never any new people that are working there. So when there is a new person, I am comfortable with saying hi, and if there is a customer that I am near, I am comfortable saying hi to them also.

My work is like a third home to me. I am comfortable there. I do the treadmill, I enjoy the work I do and the people I work with. The room that the treadmill is in is my room to put my purse and bag when I am there.

Just recently, I lost 15 pounds from not drinking soda, eating healthy, and doing the treadmill on the days I work and the bike on my days off.

Today is exactly 1 year and 2 months that I have been working at Advantage Mail.

I am a SAARCie for life!

Sara's Love Letter . . .

Hi Steve,

It has been seven years today that you passed away, and you would be proud of where our family is today. In the last seven years, we have been forced to grow stronger and stand taller in our lives. I have been blessed with so much more than I ever thought possible, especially when I was in such a bad place only seven years ago. When you died, the world became dark and full of pain, and over the years the light has slowly began to shine again.

I am happy in my life. . .finally! I once thought I would never be happy or able to live in peace and have joy, but I do and I love it! Sometimes I still get sad and cry because you are not here to see how good life is and it hurts that you only got to experience me in my rebellious teenage years. I am sorry for that. I know sadness is only something we feel on earth and you are loving your life in heaven, and that makes me happy for you.

I have come to understand that everyone and everything has to die at some point, and no matter how much my brain tells me this is the fact, my heart still is saddened by it. Mom told me she is ready to let the past be the past and to move on with our lives as whole people. We are all ready to stop hurting and start living again, no longer as broken people without a dad but strong people with a future filled with hope and possibilities. I like that idea. Seven years is a long time to hold on to the pain of losing you, and we need to be open to the future instead of scarred by the past.

My future is quite bright actually. I have a great job working at a private school as the Assistant Athletic Director. I enjoy it because I get to connect and build into students' lives every day. Not only do I have a good job, but I am also engaged and going to be married on June 22, 2012! Yes, you heard me correct — I am getting married! My fiancé's name is Aaron Weston, and we have been together for about a year and a half. We have a great life together, and it is only the beginning of all the great memories we will have together.

We are all having dinner tonight at Tarbell's to celebrate your life and start the next chapter of our lives. The next chapter in my book of life is going to be a happy one. I am excited to see what the next year brings, and I know in my heart you would be proud of me and the way my life has turned out.

Happy Daddy Day, Steve
I love you
Sara

Makena's Love Letter . . .

Dear Dad,

Wow! It has been seven years! When you left this cruel world, I was just a little five-year-old, full of anger and sadness. Over the last seven years, I have blossomed into a happy and free-spirited twelve-year-old, who is 5'9 ¾".

I love volleyball and I play on a Club team. I am a setter or middle blocker, but I just love being on the court. I love the feeling of getting a kill. I also love acting and singing. My favorite school subject is history; I think the past can help people learn about the future. Even though I love doing all these amazing things, my favorite part of volleyball, acting in plays, and learning about our miraculous past is being with my friends. They are the reason I enjoy the many activities I participate in. In volleyball, the game wouldn't exist without teammates; a good play consists of a cast, not just one person; we wouldn't have history if only one person ever lived. My friends are like the water to my seed.

Carlette, Sara, and Amanda, these are the names of three fabulous little women who have raised me. Without them, I might be the same angry little kid I was seven years ago. They give me experiences and lessons that will last a lifetime. Even though some of those lessons were hard to learn. My family is like the sunlight that feeds my little seed.

The soil is the stability that every seed or plant needs. My soil is the Lord; He is there every time I need Him. He is different from friends or family because friends can get mad, family can get frustrated, but the Lord is always standing before you with loving arms.

I love you, Daddy! Until we meet again,
Makena

I love this picture of Makena. She is so full of life and joy, open to what the world has to offer. We have all come a long way! I am in awe that it all started with Steve taking pen to paper, and many, many years later, each one of us has found our way through grief and pain to a deeper understanding of what love is, by writing our love notes to Steve.

When I think about where I am today and what I would want to write to Steve, it is simple: *I love you and thank you.*

My little women are not so little anymore, but they will forever be my little women. Their stories and their journal entries are just a little peak into their souls. I have watched them grow from sad, angry little girls to wise young women.

As we all tuck the memories of Steve deep into our hearts, I see a beautiful smile that radiates from each one of us—a smile that says we know we are loved and that we have made it through a very tough time by sticking together, clinging to our faith, and discovering what love is.

Leave it to Makena to sum it all up in a school paper that she wrote describing her life. . .

My name is Makena Patterson. I'm 12 years old, and I was born on June 18, 1999. I like to think of myself as a caring, adventurous, sporty girl who loves to laugh and have a great time. I love electronics, playing volleyball, and I absolutely love to bake. I think I get most of my traits and looks from my Dad. I miss him a lot, but at the same time I don't know really what I'm missing. I was 5 at the time he passed away, so not all my memories are very vivid of him. At the same time, I know he was a great guy and I can't wait to be with him again some day.

Even though I'm only barely 12 years old, I've had a lot of great, and what seemed at the time not so great experiences. As I'm writing this, I'm thinking back to all the "bad" experiences and I'm looking to see what was so bad about them. Let's start with the biggest and most obvious one, my Dad being dead. This experience caused me so much pain, frustration, and humiliation, but I wouldn't be the person I am today without this very important aspect in my life. I couldn't relate to other kids who have gone through the same thing. For example, this year in school, my friend's Dad passed away of cancer. This made my friend very angry and he said he felt like he didn't know where to turn, but I think having a friend with the same thing happen to them really helped my friend. He would text me almost every night with questions like, why me? Or, what should I do? I couldn't help my friend if I hadn't gone through that pain. I have also gotten to speak to adults who have kids who lost a parent and I told them what their kids might be feeling and how they could respond to their questions or tantrums.

I've also had to deal with drama that every other middle school girl has gone through — fights, transition, and bullies. Don't think that my life has been all bad, I've had so many great times, like swimming with dolphins, going on me and my mom's "cupcake tour," going to New Zealand, the list goes on and on. The moral to my story is basically your experiences make you the people you are, so don't fight them, there is always a rainbow after a storm.

I'm the author of my own life, and unfortunately, I'm writing in pen.
  - Unknown

As for all my new chapters without Steve, I have learned that the pain does not last forever, but the love we had will. What a gift.

Seven years ago, as Michelle and I sat stunned at the turn life had taken, she quietly asked me, "What do you need to get through this?" Without a moment of contemplation or hesitation, I said, "Grace!" And from that moment on, God has given me grace, taught me grace, and blessed me with grace. I had no idea what I was asking for, but God knew what I would need as I stepped into the next chapters of my life without Steve.

"Amazing grace! How sweet the sound that saved a wretch like me. I once was lost, but now am found, was blind, but now I see. Twas grace that taught my heart to fear, and grace my fears relieved. How precious did that grace appear the hour I first believed."

Today, I am forty-seven-years old and know that my forever could end at any moment. I spend my days loving my little women, working at our company, worshipping a God that I deeply love, and opening my heart to what God has planned for me. I know pain. I know hurt. I know grief.

I know love. I know God. I know grace. I know friendship. I know my truth. That's about it. I don't know what tomorrow holds, but that's fine with me because I have made peace with today.

The lives and work of the Patterson family continue. . .one day, one blessing at a time.

To be continued. . .

CHAPTER FORTY-NINE
And the Greatest of These Is Love

And the greatest of these is love.

What a gift God has given us — to know love, to feel love, to give love, to be loved. Love is the greatest of all!

I know love. I feel love when I hold my little women. I saw love when I held my dying husband. I taste love as I sip wine with my dear friends. I do wonder if I have a quota for love. Do I dare be so bold as to ask God to bless me with more love?

I feel loved in a different way. A much deeper way. I feel God's love. I feel as though Steve's love introduced me to the power of love. Only when the two loves became one did I become one with who I am. I can't give you the details of me, because I don't even know them yet, but I do recognize me. Maybe that's what love is, recognizing who God created us to be.

What a journey God has sent me on. He loved me. He created me. And then he delivered me unto this world. Ouch! I do wish he could make the transition a bit smoother. Pain. Sadness. Hurt. Struggle. I don't understand, but I trust him.

God's love is the only compass I need to find my way back to myself. He sent me here. He gave me everything that I need for my journey. He loves me. He guides me. He blesses me. And he is available to me always. For that I give thanks, and I continue on my journey until he calls me home.

My days are guided by faith, hope, and love, but the greatest of these is love.

Think back to a time when someone handed you love. . .what did you do with it?

Are you ready to fall in love with your life? I hope so.

I hope that by sharing our story, you have found the courage to share your love stories, your grief stories, and your life stories. I believe every chapter shows God's love for our lives. The good, the bad, the ugly, the sad — each chapter reveals our struggles to find peace, love, and answers to why we are here and what we are supposed to be doing with the time God grants us on earth.

I hope that you can give yourself the freedom to write the message that penetrates your heart, to the people or the person that you want to love.

I pray for you to be able to let go of the fear of what others will think. Think of all the people that have blessed your life because they were bold enough to share their heart with you. Remember all the joy felt in those amazing moments of your love story?

What would your life be like if you were living your love story?

Go ahead, fill the pages with the emotions, the people, and the love your heart longs to have written on the pages of your life. . .

I hope that you will take pen to paper or fingers to keyboard and write love notes to all the people you love. Think of how each person has blessed your life because they were bold enough to love you, and best of all, honest enough to tell you about their feelings for you.

I hope that by sharing our love story, you will be inspired to share your love story. And maybe, one love story at a time, we can soften the hearts of the world — to try love, to taste love, to embrace love, to not try to understand love but just to enjoy every minute of love.

If you would like to share your love story or how someone's love for you changed your life, go to www.loveisproject.com and bless the world with a small part of your love story. What would the world be like if we all shared what love is to us? Could we give someone who is struggling hope? Could we inspire someone who has given up to reach out to a friend? Could our simple words be the words that connected a lost soul to Jesus? We don't know, but I do know that love changed my life and my little women's life, and I am committed to helping others experience what love is. It would be an honor to have you join our family in the Love Is Project.

To read more about Steve's life and the love letters his friends and family sent to him once he became ill, go to www.stevepatterson.net.

Our family would love to hear your Daddy Day stories, or stories from your Mommy Day, or Grandma or Grandpa Day, or your Best Friend Day. Those days that they left us can become a cherished day that gives our hearts a chance to never forget how special they were to us and how their life changed our life. Go to www.daddydayalovestory.com to bless us with chapters of your journey through grief.

From our family to you, we want you to know that your life matters! Who you are, what you believe, and what your heart longs for is important. Every person, each experience, has been important in your life story. Embrace who you are and where you come from. The world needs you and everything that you stand for and want to represent. May your days be filled with love as you dive into the rest of your life. Go for it! It is so worth it!

CHAPTER FIFTY
Simple Words Worth Striving to Live By. . .1 Corinthians 13:4

- X *Love is patient*
- O Be patient as you travel on your life journey
- X *Love is kind*
- O Be kind to yourself on your journey, for your kindness will be your gift
- X *It does not envy*
- O Do not let envy take you away from your mission
- X *It does not boast*
- O Your actions will speak volumes; you will not need to say a word
- X *It is not proud*
- O Be proud of your life's work, not proud of yourself
- X *It is not rude*
- O Your heart will never be rude, but your ego can lead you astray
- X *It is not self-seeking*
- O This is about your life mission; seek to do your work, and your self will follow
- X *It is not easily angered*
- O Keep your heart and soul connected to your mission, and anger will not find a place to land
- X *It keeps no record of wrongs*
- O You won't go wrong if your life record reflects the many lives you have changed
- X *Love does not delight in evil but rejoices with the truth*
- O It is the truth that leads us to our life's work
- X *It always protects*
- O Protect your life story; you have given your life for it
- X *Always trusts*
- O Trust your desires to change the world
- X *Always hopes*
- O Hope will give you the courage to make a difference, one day at a time

X *Always perseveres*
O Only through persistence can you fulfill your life mission
X *Love never fails*
O Love what you do each day, and you won't fail to make a difference

And now these three remain:

X *Faith*
O Without it, the game is over
X *Hope*
O It is the thread that every generation weaves into the next
X *And love*
O It makes it all worthwhile
X *But the greatest of these is love*
O Give as much of it away as you can as you play this game of life, and remember, through God all things are possible!

With love,
C